Your Leadership Edge

Teacher Companion

JULIA FABRIS McBRIDE

Contents

Introduction:
Using the
Your Leadership Edge
Teacher Companion

If you teach leadership using *Your Leadership Edge: Tools and Strategies for When Everyone Leads,* this is your companion. If you are a coach or facilitator working with people who would benefit from a clear and proven approach to the activity of leadership, this is your companion. If you've attended a *Your Leadership Edge* program and want to help those you supervise embrace the principle, "leadership is an activity, not a position," this is your companion.

Two books from the Kansas Leadership Center (KLC), *Your Leadership Edge* and its prequel, *When Everyone Leads,* provide a common language and proven framework for seeing and solving our toughest challenges. Both books are highly accessible and suitable for a wide range of audiences in organizations and communities. No matter the setting, if you develop leadership capacity in others, this teacher companion empowers you to share the tools, strategies and practices from *Your Leadership Edge.*

Maybe you encountered KLC's unique leadership framework on the job, or stumbled across it online at *YourLeadershipEdge.com* or *www.Kansas LeadershipCenter.org.* Whether you are new to these leadership ideas or have been practicing and teaching them for years, this teacher companion is for you.

Perhaps you've already read *Your Leadership Edge: Tools and Strategies for When Everyone Leads* by Ed O'Malley and Amanda Cebula. Maybe you sense how powerful it would be if people at all levels in your company understood the principle that leadership is available to anyone, anytime. This teacher companion makes it easy to design training sessions or discussion groups that spread the message that we make more progress when everyone leads.

Use it as you prepare your sessions. Open it when you design classroom activities. Adapt ideas to fit your unique audiences. Carry it in your backpack when you meet with a client. Keep it on a shelf in your office or classroom. Have it handy when you teach online. Refer to it often as you coach other people to learn and use leadership skills to solve their most important challenges.

Page through it in quiet moments to keep your work grounded in the leadership framework described with such refreshing clarity in *Your Leadership Edge.*

Where These Ideas Came From

Your Leadership Edge was written by Ed O'Malley and Amanda Cebula. The leadership principles and competencies were born of intense listening and discernment by the KLC team, including the diverse and talented leadership developers whose names and influence are peppered across this companion. The ideas in *Your Leadership Edg*e have been honed over the years through experience and insight of countless people who practice leadership in Kansas and around the world.

We didn't invent the ideas. Nor were they handed down on scrolls kept by an ancient sage. They emerged from listening to people, from all walks of life, who answered the question: What kind of leadership will it take to solve our most important challenges?

Since 2007, KLC has trained thousands of people worldwide. Ranchers in Ashland, Kansas are using these leadership ideas, and so are business executives in Bangalor, London, and Melbourne. The concepts have been used to develop leadership capacity in Dakar, Senegal and to manage conflict in community meetings across Kansas and the United States.

We certainly weren't the first to talk about the concepts in this book. Ron Heifetz has been thinking about leadership as an activity, not a position, since at least 1988. Marty Linsky, Heifetz, Alexander Grashow and their colleagues at Harvard's Kennedy School and the Adaptive Leadership Network have enriched our teaching about leadership on complex, adaptive challenges. The voice of David Chrislip, coauthor of *For the Common Good: Redefining Civic Leadership,* is alive in our work, especially when we teach people to *create a trustworthy process, work across factions,* and *engage new voices.*

Toward More Open and Effective Organizations, Companies and Communities

Your Leadership Edge and its prequel *When Everyone Leads* transform the way people, organizations, and communities face tough problems.

The evidence to support the approach to leadership described in *Your Leadership Edge* is emerging in our research. (See kansasleadershipcenter.org/third-floor-research.)

Encouragingly, external evaluation of *Your Leadership Edge* and other KLC programming in 2019 by ORS Impact demonstrated that organizations and communities that saturate their systems with training such as you'll develop using this teacher companion become more open and equitable places to work or volunteer. Of course, we acknowledge the painful and deeply rooted effects that systems of oppression have had in our country and our world. We know that issues and challenges affect people differently depending on their identity, background, or status in a system. We've coached companies and organizations to use this leadership framework to face their most daunting challenges and exercise leadership to build more honest, inclusive processes and approaches. We intentionally propose *Your Leadership Edge* and *When Everyone Leads* as support for you, and your clients and students as you seek to understand systems of oppression and exercise leadership to make things better.

We All Have Aspirations

You have aspirations—for your students, your coaching clients, your community, the company you work for or own, the organization whose mission you've chosen to serve. And you know that bridging the gap between our current reality and our aspirations is going to take leadership.

Adaptive Challenges and Technical Problems

An adaptive challenge is a problem, issue or opportunity that demands a response outside your current repertoire—you don't have the information you need or a checklist you can follow to make the problem go away. Your usual tools won't work and your expertise is not enough. Addressing an adaptive challenge requires motivating people to change by engaging and challenging both their hearts and their minds. Making progress means helping people navigate loss and helping them do what is necessary instead of what is comfortable.

Most often, we try to treat adaptive challenges as if they were technical problems. Technical problems are easy to recognize, because you've seen them before. You either know the steps to solve them, or you can depend on someone else to make it happen. Technical problems live in people's heads and logic systems.

You solve technical problems by gathering facts and applying authority or expertise.

Adaptive challenges are different; they are not clearly defined and require learning to understand what is going on. The solution also requires developing new tools, methods and ways of communicating. People will need to change. Systems will need to be reinvented. Adaptive challenges live in people's hearts and stomachs. They are about values, loyalties and beliefs. Progress on adaptive challenges requires the people with the problem to do the work, and the work involves refashioning those deeply held beliefs. You can see why there is always pressure to interpret challenges as technical problems.

Most of us are not making adequate progress on the adaptive elements of the complex challenges facing our organizations and communities. Too few people are exercising leadership. Current leadership practices are inadequate. We all need to be more purposeful and provocative. We need to take more risks and engage more people.

Leadership Is an Activity

Developing leadership capacity in others begins with your decision to embrace the principle that leadership is an activity, not a position. Leadership is not a role. Leadership is distinct from authority or management. Leadership is not a set of character traits.

Leadership is mobilizing others to make progress on tough, adaptive challenges. Leadership is a series of actions and reactions designed to make progress and solve tough, entrenched challenges and to achieve bold aspirations.

Leadership requires self-awareness and ability to manage yourself so that you can effectively diagnose the challenge in front of you, energize others to care about it too, listen and integrate their perspectives, and intervene skillfully enough to make progress on something important for the common good.

The five leadership principles listed on pages 8 and 9 of this teacher companion represent fundamental beliefs about leadership. They describe the kind of leadership it takes to make progress on our toughest challenges. To teach or coach using the ideas from *Your Leadership Edge* and to make full use of this companion, you'll need to embrace those five principles, starting with adopting the perspective that *leadership is an activity, not a position.*

As you design and deliver sessions using this teacher companion, and as you encourage learners to experiment with ideas from *Your Leadership Edge,* weave in multiple discussions about this first leadership principle. Help people integrate it with their personal worldviews. Without embracing the idea that leadership is an activity, it is difficult to fully utilize the ideas and tools from *Your Leadership Edge*. For a deeper dive into the leadership principles and the vision behind *Your Leadership Edge,* have your students read *When Everyone Leads: How Tough Challenges Get Seen and Solved.*

DEFINITIONS

Leadership is mobilizing people to make progress on complex challenges.

Authority is a contract to provide protection, direction and order in exchange for collaboration. When the work is technical, authority may be sufficient for success.

Leadership is an activity while authority is a position. Anyone can lead, including people in authority. Leadership from a position of authority comes with unique constraints and possibilities.

Progress means forward movement on an adaptive challenge and is the desired outcome of an act of leadership. Progress is not always immediately evident. Progress may include learning or insight, including from an intervention that did not go as planned.

When Everyone Leads

We hope you see your own experience reflected in these pages. With this book as your companion, you can have even more impact in the months and years to come. As someone who teaches or coaches using *Your Leadership Edge,* you play a key role in an unfolding story of more and more people hearing the call to leadership and assuming responsibility for building a better world. Each person you reach gets us closer to our shared goal of healthier, stronger businesses, organizations, and communities. With you as our partner, we envision a future where people everywhere embrace the notion that leadership is an activity, not a position. We envision a future when everyone leads. Thank you for all you are doing to transform civic culture by equipping and empowering others to engage in the activity of leadership. Together we'll solve our most important challenges and create lasting, positive change in our organizations, companies, and communities.

Let These Principles Guide Your Way

Principle #1:
Leadership is an activity, not a position.

Leadership and authority are two different things. *Leadership* is mobilizing others to solve their most important challenges. *Authority* is more like management. Having good people in authority positions is absolutely necessary to keep things functioning at a high level, but authority alone is not sufficient to make progress on the things that matter most.

Principle #2:
Anyone can lead, anytime, anywhere.

If we want to solve our most important challenges, more people need to embrace the idea that everyone can lead. When it comes to our toughest challenges, we all have a part to play. Lots of people need to contribute time and energy. Saying "yes" to the idea that anyone can see and seize their moment to lead means risking your own comfort for the sake of progress on something that matters.

Principle #3:
Leadership starts with you and must engage others.

Some things an expert can fix or the boss can order done. But as a culture, we've fallen into the bad habit of waiting for others to lead. When you embrace this principle, the waiting is over. Action is yours to take and the time is now. No matter your position, age, or level of experience, you can do something to mobilize others to make progress on an important leadership challenge. The goal of taking action is not to fix things yourself but to engage other people.

Principle #4:
Leadership is risky.

If you've ever attempted to get people to work together on a difficult challenge, you know that leadership is risky. We want to drive home this principle as both a warning and encouragement. Even as you do everything you can to energize others to solve a big challenge, pay attention and build your skill at minimizing risks.

Principle #5:
Leadership is about our toughest challenges.

You have to care about something really important—an aspiration or a big concern. Without a clear sense of purpose nothing is going to change. It's not leadership if it's not about those tough challenges.

Leadership Competencies and Dimensions

Back in 2007, when KLC was getting started, we asked people: What kind of leadership does it take to make progress on the deep, daunting challenges that serve as barriers to a healthier, stronger, more prosperous state? Responses fell into four simple yet profound categories. We call those categories the leadership competencies. The bullets underneath, we call the dimensions.

Diagnose Situation

- Distinguish technical and adaptive work
- Understand the process challenges
- Explore tough interpretations
- Take the temperature
- Identify who needs to do the work
- Test multiple interpretations

Manage Self

- Manage your vulnerabilities and triggers
- Get used to uncertainty and conflict
- Choose among competing values
- Know the stories others tell about you
- Experiment beyond your comfort zone
- Take care of yourself

Energize Others

- Engage new voices
- Start where they are
- Work across factions
- Create a trustworthy process
- Speak to loss
- Inspire a collective purpose

Intervene Skillfully

- Make purposeful choices
- Raise the heat
- Speak from the heart to the heart
- Give the work back
- Act experimentally
- Hold to purpose

The dimensions are the best descriptions we have of what the activity of leadership looks like. While in this book we sometimes use the words "dimension" and "behavior" interchangeably, the dimensions are not discrete action steps. Rather, they are signposts pointing to a set of potential actions, behaviors or experiments. The dimensions bring to life our definition of leadership as mobilizing people to make progress on complex challenges.

This teacher companion aligns precisely with *Your Leadership Edge* by Ed O'Malley and Amanda Cebula. It contains 24 chapters. This introduction covers the leadership principles. Subsequent chapters cover the dimensions in the order they are listed on page 10. Each chapter features:

- **Two sets of learning objectives.**
- **References to resources** (books, downloads, etc.) with specific page numbers from *Your Leadership Edge* and links to use in your teaching or coaching.
- **Clues, tips and examples** from the KLC team.
- **Space in the margins** for you to reflect, plan and jot down ideas.

Our big purpose with this book is to state what's essential about our framework, giving you a strong foundation on which to innovate.

Level 1 and Level 2 Objectives

We define "objective" as what you intend to have happen for the learner as a result of your leadership development intervention. In each chapter you'll find two sets of objectives. Broadly speaking, successfully fulfilling Level 1 objectives prepares a learner to tackle Level 2 objectives.

Level 1 objectives target learners and coaching clients who are new to the *Your Leadership Edge* ideas or just opening their minds to a certain aspect of leadership. Level 1 objectives are about seeing the world in a different way; they are about testing new behaviors and adopting the principle that leadership is an activity, available to anyone, anytime, anywhere. Level 1 objectives help people build courage and get enough practice with a certain leadership behavior to try a few new moves back at home.

Build your leadership development experiences around specific objectives. Don't attempt to cover all the Level 1 objectives associated with a dimension, for instance, in one sitting. Our experience shows people understand and apply ideas more readily when we have fewer objectives. So, if you are teaching, *explore multiple interpretations,* don't attempt to cover all Level 1 objectives related to that dimension. Likewise, address foundational objectives first. Allow learners to integrate Level 1 objectives into their understanding and practice of leadership before challenging them with Level 2.

Level 2 objectives take the learning and application deeper. In many cases, they take teachers and learners beyond the scope of what's contained in *Your Leadership Edge.* They require more risk, more discomfort, more opportunities to look incompetent. Sessions and experiences you'll design using Level 2 objectives encourage people to face themselves honestly, to explore ways they may need to change their behavior. Level 2 objectives amp up the emphasis on practice. They push people to engage with others in a classroom and back in their context. Level 2 objectives revolve around real-world adaptive challenges and the learner's growing capacity to hold to purpose long enough to energize others and make substantial progress.

Types of Objectives

Within each level are three types of objectives. While we warn you against trying to cover all the objectives related to a given dimension in a single session, the most powerful learning experiences tend to involve one of each of these three types.

- **Knowledge objectives.** (What do we want people to learn, understand or explore?)
- **Experience objectives.** (What do we want people to feel or realize? What attitude shift are we aiming for?)
- **Action objectives.** (What do we want people to do or practice, either right away or after the experience?)

Go ahead and copy and paste objectives from this book into your syllabi and program plans. As you do so, note that in several places we've included in parentheses a little extra explanation of the objective. You can choose whether to share that with your participants in writing, verbally, or simply to have it in the back of your mind as you teach.

Leadership is an activity best learned by doing. Many times you will choose to challenge people to put an idea into practice right in the classroom, using case-in-point or some other form of experiential learning. Other times you will prepare people and assign homework that allows them to fulfill the objective back at home. You may design homework to provoke learning and action outside the classroom. Often, a provocative question or subtle challenge is all it takes.

Before You Teach, Get Grounded

Teaching to the objectives outlined in this book requires a thorough knowledge and robust practice of the leadership principles and competencies introduced in *Your Leadership Edge.* To ethically and effectively teach or coach you need to know and use the ideas yourself. Some people get a good grounding in the leadership framework by reading *Your Leadership Edge* and *When Everyone Leads: How Tough Challenges Get Seen and Solved.* Alternatively, you can complete the 25 asynchronous modules at *yourleadershipedge.com* and take the accompanying skills quizzes. If you are able, we encourage you to complete KLC's Your Leadership Edge program virtually or in person. Then, go deeper with Lead for Change, KLC's course designed around Level 2 objectives in this book. Then you can focus on developing your teaching and coaching skills in our Teach Leadership, Leadership Coach and Advanced Leadership Development intensives. As you read this book, be prepared to cross-reference with *Your Leadership Edge* and online content indicated in each chapter.

In the KLC Store at *kansasleadershipcenter.org/klcstore* you'll find worksheets and other materials you can pass on to students and coaching clients. Or ask them to purchase the *KLC Guidebook,* frequently referenced here.

Fit Objectives to Your Audience

As you craft your leadership development experiences, consider your audience first. Choose objectives to fit their needs. Pace the work. Don't try to cram it all into one session. Know your audience, then design activities and identify resources to fit your time and aspirations.

Knowing your audience includes getting as familiar as you can with the individuals and groups within the larger groups. Who will you be working with? What unique challenges does each person or group face? What could make it difficult for them to learn in your setting?

What do you know about backgrounds and social identities? Will they immediately see you as someone who is on your side, or has their experience made them skeptical of experts, or words like "leadership" or "experiment"? Who is likely to feel immediately comfortable in the setting you create? Who is not?

Learn as much as you can in advance about the varying levels of experience, privilege, caution, and confidence in the room. From there, do your best to create, if not a level playing field, then the scaffolding necessary for everyone to enter in, find their place, learn and grow through their experience.

Get Creative with Your Session Design

At the end of each chapter you'll find a section titled Session Design Ideas (You Take it From Here). At first, you may find those ideas maddeningly incomplete. We hope, on second reading, you'll find they inspire creativity. They are intended as the first germ of an idea to get you started. Think about your audience, choose your objectives and see if one of the suggestions has any juice. Or let our ideas jump start your brainstorming and challenge you to come up with something better. While our design suggestions are written with classroom teachers in mind, coaches and managers may find inspiration there for between-meeting assignments.

In addition to session objectives and design ideas, each chapter features important definitions, visuals and charts related to the leadership dimension. You'll also find examples of leadership behaviors in action in the section titled In the Real World, plus frequently asked questions and wisdom from KLC team members for you to weave in or adapt for your audience.

The Stake-in-the-Ground Paradox

On the one hand, this book is meant to put a stake in the ground about how to teach the contents of *Your Leadership Edge.* On the other hand, this book is meant to encourage creativity: For instance, if we've listed six Level 1 learning objectives for a certain dimension, we hope you'll add a seventh. If we've identified links between that dimension and four other ideas from *Your Leadership Edge,* we know you'll find three more. While we've found additional grounding for these leadership competencies in the work of Eric Lui and Brené Brown and others, we know you'll find your own routes to landing the ideas with the people you teach and coach.

The Stake-in-the-Ground Paradox works like this: See the stake in the ground. Respect it. Know we put it there for good reason. Show other people the stake. Learn all you can about why we've put it where we've put it. Then, if you feel like it, move the stake.

Reading this Book

While a few hardy souls may wish to read this book from cover to cover, you have full permission to skip ahead to the chapters you need right away. Wherever you start, read with a pencil in hand, ready to fill in the blank spaces designed to prompt you to think of examples and note ideas that will be useful in your session design.

Your Lifetime Replacement Policy

It is our hope that you will handle this book every day. We want you to mark it up, flag pages, fold corners, spill coffee on it, and stuff the book into already over-full bags and briefcases. Thus, we offer you a lifetime replacement policy. When it gets too messy to enjoy, or when your colleagues turn away in disgust when you pull it out, let us know and we will send you another copy free of charge.

Author's Voice and Aspirations

Though one person (Julia Fabris McBride) wrote this book and is responsible for all gaps, faults and errors, the KLC team together created what is of value here. Therefore, we use the first-person plural throughout. We learned so much in the creation of this book that has already improved our teaching and coaching. We hope you find it as useful and inspiring as we do.

> **"When I am coaching people who assume they do not have sufficient positional authority to mobilize others, I challenge them on two fronts: One is about credibility. You may not have the position, but you may have credibility from experience, expertise, or relationships. You may have more leverage than you think. The second front is about partnering with authority. OK, you aren't in the position to mobilize people. Who is? How can you influence or gain the trust of that authority holder?"**
>
> **Seth Bate, PCC, KLC Teacher and Coach**

PART ONE

DIAGNOSE SITUATION

Developing leadership capacity in others starts with helping them see that to make more progress on tough issues they need to hone their diagnostic skills.

Leadership requires understanding the context and nuances of the challenge they are dealing with. For starters, they've got to identify the problem correctly—technical, adaptive or both? Then, they'll need to consider multiple perspectives and explanations about what's going on.

Making systemic and what we call "tough-on-me" interpretations means pushing beyond conclusions and opinions that come automatically, almost unconsciously. Press your students to get curious. Encourage them to be more skeptical (or keep an open mind). They may need to thoughtfully question the perspective of the person in authority. They may need to look at the situation from someone else's point of view. Good diagnosis means thinking more about process than content.

Good diagnosis means thinking more about how you are going to engage others than about marshaling the facts and making the best argument. Teach them to take the temperature. Help them practice looking for conflict or pain, where the heat is in the system, where the disequilibrium is high, or where people are bored or checked out. All of those signal the need for leadership.

The more they diagnose, the more options they have for action. The more they get to know the problem, the more opportunities they'll have to solve it.

CHAPTER 1

Distinguish Technical and Adaptive Work

The leadership competencies are tools and strategies for when everyone leads. They are built to help people make progress on adaptive challenges. Big daunting challenges require curiosity and learning, so we have the competency Diagnose Situation; adaptive work can't be accomplished by authorities alone, so we have to Energize Others; when the work is adaptive, we experiment and making progress through behaviors listed under Intervene Skillfully; and adaptive work is long-term, slow work with lots of ups and downs, so we have to attend to the competency of Manage Self all along the way. This chapter covers the first dimension, *distinguish technical and adaptive work*, of the first competency, Diagnose Situation.

Your Leadership Edge p 14–21

• • • • •

We rarely design even a short leadership program that does not include at least a review or broad strokes introduction of this idea. With intact teams and groups from the same organization we almost always introduce *distinguish technical and adaptive* work within the first hour of being together. We introduce our leadership framework, and set people up to use the tools and strategies from *Your Leadership Edge,* by making the case that there is a gap between their current situation and concerns and where they want to be, and that the challenges getting in their way will not be solved by business as usual. We introduce the definitions and distinctions between technical problems and adaptive challenges and, drawing on their examples, demonstrate that the challenges holding them back are adaptive. We make the case that when everyone in their system thinks about leadership differently and sees their role in adaptive work, they can expect better results and achieve their aspirations sooner.

Since *distinguish technical and adaptive work* is fundamental to everything we teach and since it has so many nuances, this is the only chapter of the *Your Leadership Edge Teacher Companion* in which we present our Level 1 objectives in three categories: Know, Experience, and Do. (Remember, a good approach when designing your session is to include an objective from each of the three categories. Adults learn from reflecting on experience. Build in time for both action and reflection.)

While we start most programs with this dimension of Diagnose Situation, we have found that for people with no formal authority and little sense of personal agency this idea sometimes falls flat. They can't see themselves as having a role in adaptive work or the capacity to engage in leadership as an activity. For them, it may be most useful to start your introduction to this new approach to leadership with the competency Manage Self. Once they've become acquainted with the idea of a comfort zone and what it might be like to experiment with something other than their default behaviors, thought about how to manage the inevitable triggers, and begun to entertain the idea of getting used to uncertainty and discomfort for the sake of something they care about, they will be more ready to imagine their own role in work.

> **"It's our human tendency to want to apply technical fixes to adaptive issues. That leads to frustration in organizations. The fixes don't work and progress stalls. A critical part of diagnosing the situation is identifying what's adaptive and what's not. When coaching, I'll often ask, 'What's hitting you in the gut right now?' That question is a shortcut to, 'What's adaptive?'"**
>
> **Tina Khan, KLC Teacher and Civic Facilitator**

DEFINITIONS

Technical problems can be solved by experts or authority, fewer people may be needed. Someone has solved the problem before and a road map for next steps exists.

Adaptive challenges require new learning about what the problem is and how best to proceed. Stakeholders from a variety of factions must be engaged, and people must experiment to test possible ways of moving forward and making progress.

	TECHNICAL	ADAPTIVE
PROBLEM	clear	requires learning
SOLUTION	clear	requires learning
WHOSE WORK IS IT?	experts, authority	stakeholders
TYPE OF WORK	efficient	act experimentally
TIMELINE	ASAP	longer term
EXPECTATIONS	fix problem	make progress
ATTITUDE	confidence, skill	curiosity

Objectives

LEVEL 1

At Level 1 learners need to have five things about adaptive and technical work solidly in their heads.

1. **Know** the definitions of technical problems and adaptive challenges and confidently describe the difference between the two.

2. **Understand** why technical fixes don't work when what we are facing is an adaptive challenge. (And with that perhaps feel some relief along the lines of "Whew. It's not that I'm incompetent, it's that I didn't take the time to understand what I was dealing with.")

3. **Understand** how to apply the distinctions to our own challenges using questions like, "What aspects of this situation are technical? What can be solved by bringing in the right expert or spending money in the right place?And what is adaptive here? What do we need to learn?"

4. **Know** why this idea is so important to the exercise of leadership. (If the work is technical, you can use your authority or leverage someone else's. If it's adaptive you need to lead. You need to use behaviors described in *Your Leadership Edge* to mobilize other people to make progress. There is no solving, or even making progress on, adaptive challenges without leadership.)

5. **Internalize** the definition of leadership as mobilizing people to make progress on tough, daunting, adaptive challenges.

Knowing is not enough, however. Experiencing the distinction between technical and adaptive challenges at a gut level is key if we want to motivate people to lead. Here's what we want going on in the hearts of our participants as they complete Level 1.

6. **Experience** a new energy and sense of possibility. (See their problems differently. Get why they've been stuck or going in circles. A light bulb goes on: "Of course! That's why I haven't been able to make change.")

7. **Feel** anxious or overwhelmed as the reality sinks in about how difficult adaptive work really is.

8. **Feel** excitement in beginning to see the leadership principles and competencies as clues to a new way forward on adaptive challenges.

Of course, none of this knowing and feeling means anything unless it leads to action. When people at Level 1 go back into the world they need to do something different.

9. **See** our own systems differently (perhaps as a place where people do whatever is necessary to avoid adaptive work).

10. **Use** creative, curious questions to help others see the complex, adaptive nature of challenges around them.

11. **Explain** the distinction between technical and adaptive work to colleagues and help others discern when authority and expertise are sufficient to move a project forward, and when some other approach (like leadership) is needed.

12. **Spend** more time in diagnosis to thoroughly understand technical and adaptive elements of a situation.

LEVEL 2

1. **Understand** that the leadership competencies from *Your Leadership Edge* are built to help us make progress on adaptive challenges.

2. **Know** how to use the distinctions between technical and adaptive to make and test tougher interpretations.

3. **Experience** the systemic pressure to treat every problem like it is technical (and fixable by the right authority or expert).

4. **Intervene** differently, purposefully and more often to make progress on adaptive challenges using the range of behaviors described in *Your Leadership Edge*.

Q&A

Q: How can I fully communicate to a group (or coaching client for that matter) the difference between technical issues and adaptive challenges?

A: Get them to consider where the two types of problems reside in their bodies. We like to use the terms "neck up" and "neck down" to distinguish these differences with a group. Technical issues exist from the neck up; we process and think about them at a head level. Adaptive challenges, on the other hand, live below the neck, in our heart and gut. For some people, it's adaptive if thinking about it gives them a stomachache.

In the real world

In K-12 education, it's technical work to translate the student handbook into all the languages spoken in the district. It gets adaptive to make sure families who speak languages other than English, and who come from cultures with unique sets of values, understand how to access available services and come to terms with what is most important for their children to succeed in school.

In a health care agency, mapping the organizational chart and who reports to whom is technical work. But when a nurse gets promoted to CEO over a doctor who also applied for the job, the work to build trust among staff is adaptive.

To successfully design and implement diversity, equity, and inclusion initiatives, an organization must distinguish the desired outcomes from the more adaptive process goals. It is technical work to name organizational outcome goals (i.e., to increase BIPOC hires, promote more women, etc.). It is adaptive to fully understand the organization's level of readiness to implement those goals and begin to surface the unspoken fears among staff. (i.e., How will new hires thrive in the existing environments? Will promoted individuals be supported and respected in their new roles?)

Edison Trickett in *The American Journal of Community Psychology* recounts the story of public health workers in 1955 who assumed that if they provided enough information about the health risks of drinking water straight from the stream Peruvian women would start boiling water. The health workers treated water-related illness as a technical challenge their expertise would be sufficient to solve. It didn't work. The women did not change their habits. What if, instead of launching into directions for boiling water, the health workers had stepped into the women's daily routines to explore barriers and possibilities? What if they'd expressed curiosity about the cultural meaning of hot and cold water? What if they'd embraced the adaptive elements of eliminating water-related risks?

Resources

Your Leadership Edge, pages 14–21.

When Everyone Leads, *Part One: Identify the Gap.*

KLC Guidebook, page 11, *Sequencing Powerful Questions.*

KLC Guidebook, pages 22 and 23.

Teaching Leadership: Case-in-Point, Case Studies and Coaching, coaching questions on page 168, *Life in the Gap,* page 198–202.

Video – Adaptive vs. Technical
go.kansasleadershipcenter.org/AVT

Cartoons – Diagnose Situation Package
go.kansasleadershipcenter.org/CT_DS

Worksheets – Diagnose Situation Package
go.kansasleadershipcenter.org/WS_DS

Work across factions (a dimension of Energize Others) is integral to adaptive work. If you need to engage people who don't think like you, the work is adaptive, not technical.

Speak to loss (another dimension of Energize Others) means helping people navigate the loss that comes with change. There will always be downsides to progress when the work is adaptive.

Session ideas

1.

Assign individuals to describe a challenge in writing. Prompt them with questions like: What is a problem, challenge or opportunity you'd like to make more progress on? What is the background? Why is it important to you? What actions have you taken so far? What do you intend to do in the future? In what ways are you stuck or confused? Invite a volunteer to read their challenge aloud. Using the chart on page 23 to frame the discussion, coach the group to identify technical and adaptive elements of the challenge.

2.

Using the group in your classroom as a case, offer your opinion that they share an assumed common purpose. They all want to learn and practice leadership skills. Coax them to articulate the work they'll need to do to be successful, and to distinguish the adaptive and technical aspects of that work.

CHAPTER 2

Understand the Process Challenges

We often teach this dimension of Diagnose Situation, *understand the process challenges,* in concert with the Energize Others dimension *create a trustworthy process.* We teach it in our second level leadership development programs because it requires a keen grasp of the distinction between adaptive challenges and technical problems that can only be gained through seeing the world through that lens. This aspect of Diagnose Situation can bring a much needed injection of hope and new things to pay attention to for those who have experienced the difficulty of attempting to get diverse factions to work together when the work is adaptive.

Your Leadership Edge p 22-29

As you teach the dimension *understand the process challenges* keep reminding yourself that this behavior falls under the competency of Diagnose Situation. *Understand the process challenges* means examining the ways those with convening authority attempt to bring people together to do difficult work. Their process could be a premeditated, purposefully designed, even rigid series of steps and activities. Or it may be a more experimental approach dependent on constant observation, interpretations, and adjustments along the way. With adaptive work, teach your students that they'll likely need a combination of both a purposeful plan and an experimental mindset ready to adapt to the needs of stakeholders and preferences of the factions you need to engage.

Understand the process challenges also requires attending to peoples' experience of and reaction to the way you approach and seek to engage them in the challenge. The best laid plans will fail to successfully energize people if key individuals or factions decide they don't trust the process. Likewise, full understanding of process challenges requires curiosity about relationships and the interpersonal feelings, opinions, loyalties, and habits at work in the system one hopes to change.

This dimension of Diagnose Situation prepares people to identify emotionally intelligent approaches to difficult work. Remind those you seek to develop that adaptive work will almost always involve some conflict, loss, risk, discomfort, and the need to let go of old ways before we know for sure what the new ways will be.

Encourage your students to assume, when facing an adaptive challenge, that process challenges will start at the very beginning with defining the problem. The problem may look completely different to one faction than to another. What process challenges are they likely to face, with their particular adaptive challenge, as they acknowledge the differing perspectives of the people they need to energize?

A final introductory note: Be thoughtful when talking about this dimension in industry settings. Among some software engineers, for instance, a "process challenge" means something closer to what we would call a technical challenge. That is, it is a problem that can be traced to a particular step in a product delivery process and a particular person or team owns that step. In such a setting, emphasize that this dimension is about how people are working together rather than simply where the issue is located.

> **"Coaching clients will frequently express a challenge by naming a solution they already have in mind. ('The problem is we need to educate people about the best approach.' 'The problem is we need buy-in for the new vision.') This is a signal to ask about the problem beneath the problem—and potentially the problem beneath that problem. Process challenges run deep."**
>
> **Seth Bate, PCC, KLC Teacher and Coach**

DEFINITIONS

Content challenges are the nuts and bolts. They are the things you know how to do or can get trained to accomplish, things you can touch or point to, decisions that entail a choice among clear options.

Process challenges are issues or barriers among the individuals, factions and systems who must navigate change or work together to make progress on an adaptive challenge.

Content Challenges

- The problem as stated, usually in technical terms
- Nuts and bolts decisions and details
- Data, reports, plans
- Known options
- Association with experts
- Face value

Process Challenges

- The problem behind the problem
- How people work or don't work together
- Patterns in systems
- Competing values/priorities
- Think "adaptive"
- Possible "surprises" that might derail us?
- What needs attention now, later?

Objectives

LEVEL 1

1. **Know** the definitions of and difference between content challenges and process challenges.

2. **Understand** the role of authority to set the stage for effective, trustworthy processes.

3. **Demonstrate** ability to diagnose real-world process challenges by exploring the various values, loyalties, opinions, relationships, feelings, etc. that could get in the way of progress (what we call the "problems behind the problem").

4. **Identify** what is going well with a process, and where there are barriers.

5. **Anticipate** process challenges from multiple perspectives, and from beyond our own needs, expectations and desires.

LEVEL 2

1. **Understand** that one of the hallmarks of adaptive work is that a trustworthy, effective and inclusive process is required to make progress and find solutions.

2. **Elevate** process to a conscious level. (Changing a system or culture requires being able to talk about existing norms and what you want to be different.)

3. **Intervene** in the moment to offer ways to improve the group's process of working together.

In the real world

A multi-site company struggles to build a cohesive culture after a merger. Even the technical work of scheduling meetings is rife with conflict as units in different time zones engage in a silent push and pull about whose business day will be the standard.

In a nonprofit organization, who sets the board meeting agendas? Who decides how long meetings last? How much meaningful responsibility do board volunteers have? These questions reveal processes that are working, and process challenges that reduce the effectiveness of board members.

A company aspires to hire more people of color. They contract with a diversity and equity consultant who shares best practices and leaves them with a new plan for posting, interviewing and hiring. But the process doesn't work as they'd hoped, perhaps because it did not do enough to change habits and mitigate implicit biases of the people doing the interviewing.

Q&A

Q: What's the difference between an adaptive challenge and a process challenge?

A: One way to think about it is that a big, daunting adaptive challenge includes process challenges, manage-self challenges, purpose-related challenges, and even technical challenges. Understanding the process challenges is one lens through which to diagnose the problem.

Resources

Your Leadership Edge, pages 22–29.

When Everyone Leads, *Part Two: Barriers to Progress.*

KLC Guidebook, pages 57–61 and page 68. Observations at the interpersonal and system level can help participants notice ongoing processes, and the "Explore Process" questions can help assess process challenges (page 59).

Cartoons – Diagnose Situation Package
go.kansasleadershipcenter.org/CT_DS

Tema Okun's culture descriptions and assessments can help people who design processes make choices that are more consciously equitable and inclusive. Unconsciously adopting the white cultural norms expressed in perfectionism, urgency, and the worship of the written word may lead to less inclusive, effective processes that normalize whiteness and marginalize voices and experiences of people of color. See go.kansasleadershipcenter.org/culture for one useful introduction.

Leadership ideas with direct links to process challenges include work *across factions* (Energize Others), *raise the heat* (Intervene Skillfully), and *get used to uncertainty and conflict* (Manage Self). If you try to convene factions for dialogue or constructive work, you'll need a process that honors their divergent values and points of view. That requires you to *create a trustworthy process* (Energize Others). Likewise, it requires skillful intervention to get the right people feeling enough heat to move, but not so much that they abandon the work. Creating space to name and address the process challenges requires preparing self and others to navigate conflicting points of view and uncertainty about the direction conversations will take.

Session ideas

1.

Have the group use the Create a Trustworthy Process tool on page 82 of the *KLC Guidebook* to diagnose the process challenges in your classroom.

2.

If your program includes assessments such as Kolbe, Myers-Briggs, or DiSC, use the results to identify potential process challenges. For instance, people who have one preference may naturally start addressing an adaptive challenge by brainstorming the most inspiring ideas, while people with a different preference may begin by using budget data to set parameters.

3.

Between sessions, invite people to complete page 68 in the *KLC Guidebook,* listing process challenges they are facing. Support them in developing a plan to address the top one or two challenges they identify.

CHAPTER 3

Explore Tough Interpretations

"Ooh, a blindfold—what fun! But where's the piñata?"

One big barrier to effective leadership is our human disinclination to consider points of view other than our own. Another barrier is the high-functioning person's understandable desire to solve problems quickly and without engaging the necessary stakeholders. As teachers and coaches, we need to push people to view their leadership challenges from multiple perspectives. Only then can they begin to *explore tough interpretations* about the situation and imagine the work it will take to create and sustain change.

→ Your Leadership Edge p 30–35

We introduce this dimension of Diagnose Situation, *explore tough interpretations,* early in most KLC programs and it involves teaching no less than eight important definitions. See page 41. Three of these words (observation, interpretation, intervention) are used in our curriculum to describe the process of seeing a system or situation, recognizing a challenge that requires leadership and taking action to change things for the better. One defines systems. Four others describe types of interpretations useful to consider when exercising leadership.

Granted, eight is a lot of definitions to throw at people who are new to thinking about leadership as mobilizing people to do difficult work. Fortunately, you can simplify. To do that, get very clear about the objectives you'll cover and design your approach to fit the group. Then, instead of dwelling on confusing new terms and definitions, focus on communicating three key things. Tell your students:

- You won't make good interpretations unless you slow down and make observations first;
- We humans are drawn toward the easy interpretations; and
- It's only when we push ourselves to make tougher interpretations that we can identify interventions (aka experiments or action steps) that will shake things up enough to create change.

Exploring tough interpretations gives you the perspective you need to design interventions that compel people to work together differently.

Give people the definitions but don't dwell on them or get too caught up in making sure people understand the distinctions perfectly. To accommodate visual learners (and there are a lot of them in every room) give the definitions in writing—on a slide, in the *KLC Guidebook,* or on a handout. But as you dig into this dimension, replace the big words with time to practice letting go of reliance on easy interpretations in favor of exploring the tough ones. At KLC, we always use visuals when we introduce this dimension. Show the chart at the bottom of page 44 and encourage people to make interpretations that fit the definitions on the right (tougher) side of the chart.

As you move into teaching the Level 2 objectives here, you'll discover that making tough interpretations forces us to think systemically. It jolts us out of a paradigm in which even the most competent individual can direct the outcomes, and into the world of complex, intersecting, overlapping, and conflicting pressures, needs and aspirations. *Explore multiple interpretations* is a diagnostic behavior that prepares us for situations where people with differing perspectives must find ways to work together to create sustainable change.

"It is surprisingly common for people in positions of authority to stay fixed on their initial interpretation of a problem rather than consider a broader range of possibilities. As an executive coach I find it is useful for clients to pause and entertain interpretations beyond their own before making important decisions. This enables them to move past the reflexive tendency to act quickly. They make better choices and move forward more effectively."

Tim Link, MA, MCC, KLC Director of Coach Training

DEFINITIONS

Observation is the action or process of noticing the details, events and patterns in the system you are trying to change (including data from your own body).

Interpretation is the action or process of assigning meaning or making sense of something you observe.

Intervention is the action or process of attempting to change a system or gather additional data, often referred to as an experiment or an act of leadership.

A **system** is a collection of parts intended to accomplish an overall mission, purpose, or integrated set of goals. In organizational and community life, absent a culture of leadership at all levels, a system is more likely to react to unstated internal or external pressures than to function effectively to meet its stated purpose.

Easy-on-me interpretations don't challenge the status quo or the story we like to tell about our own exercise of leadership. They fit in the easy interpretation category.

Individual interpretations account for actions by assigning cause to a specific individual. They fit in the easy interpretation category.

Tough-on-me interpretations raise the heat (cause discomfort) by revealing unspoken motivations and "our part of the mess." They implicate the person (or persons) seeking to exercise leadership. They fit in the tough interpretation category.

Systemic interpretations account for pressures, patterns and roles that exist in any group. They fit in the tough interpretation category.

Objectives

LEVEL 1

1. **Know** the definitions of observation, interpretation and intervention.

2. **Understand** definitions of and distinctions among four types of interpretations (see pages 41 and 44).

3. **Experience** how challenging and contrary it is to typical norms of polite conversation to share tough-on-me and systemic interpretations out loud in a group.

4. **Experience** availability of more options for intervention when a group allows itself to entertain multiple and tough interpretations.

5. **Practice** generating multiple interpretations that are tougher and more systemic.

LEVEL 2

1. **Understand** that since leadership happens in systems it is worth taking time to dig deep into diagnosis of systemic patterns, pressures, power and processes.

2. **Know** the definition of system.

3. **Understand** the consequences of not exploring systemic interpretations.

4. **Recognize** that inequity dynamics (e.g., racism, ageism, sexism, ableism, etc.) are always at play in systems and be prepared to elevate them whenever they stand as impediments to leadership and progress.

5. **Explore** the context in which your adaptive challenge exists and understand the systemic structures that may leave some people behind.

6. **Complete** a deep diagnosis and map of the system surrounding your adaptive challenge. (Use open-ended questions about patterns, pressures, power, and process.)

7. **Invite** people from diverse factions surrounding your challenge to share tough-on-me and systemic interpretations.

8. **Practice** engaging a team in making tough interpretations even if they are not well-versed in the ideas from *Your Leadership Edge.*

Make Tough Interpretations

Easy-On-Me: Interpretations that don't challenge the status quo or the story we like to tell.	>>	**Tough-On-Me:** Raises the heat by revealing unspoken motivations and "our part of the mess."
Individual: Accounting for actions by assigning cause to a specific individual.	>>	**Systemic:** Accounts for pressures, patterns and roles that exist in any group.

In the real world

A nonprofit executive notices that she no longer looks forward to going to work. Lingering at a nearby coffee shop she catalogs her observations: Colleagues are routinely late for work, sometimes even missing the first half of a weekly all-staff meeting. People rarely lift a head to say good morning or go out to lunch together anymore. She concludes that the culture is suffering and pushes herself to explore multiple interpretations about the cause. In the easy-on-me category, she lists, "People are exhausted after a string of high-pressure events," and in the individual interpretation category, "Staff members need to get better at taking care of themselves." Then, sensing there is more to it, the exec pushes herself to consider harder-to-deal with interpretations like, "I am not modeling healthy behavior," and "We've lost our collective sense of purpose."

Q&A

Q: In the classroom, how do I get people to share their diverse or conflicting interpretations?

A: First, connect the work to a larger purpose: We need more people exercising more leadership more effectively. Then, acknowledge how hard leadership can be. Leadership is risky, every time, everywhere. Life offers daily invitations to navigate that risk for the sake of contributing in more meaningful ways. Alternatively, just name what you are noticing: "I'm experiencing that the group is having a hard time naming tough interpretations. Does anyone feel the same?" If participants are still slow to practice tough interpretations, consider shifting the work to the realm of Manage Self. People are more willing to name tough interpretations if you pair it with practice managing triggers and vulnerabilities.

Resources

Your Leadership Edge, pages 30–35.

When Everyone Leads, chapter 21, *Everyone Can Make Multiple Interpretations*.

KLC Guidebook, pages 16–17 and pages 32–33 (level 1) and pages 57–61 (level 2).

Video – "Explore Multiple Interpretations"
go.kansasleadershipcenter.org/EMI

Cartoons – Diagnose Situation Package
go.kansasleadershipcenter.org/CT_DS

Bob Kegan and Lisa Lahey's work on *Immunity to Change* is all about helping people see multiple perspectives. As our minds grow from one stage of adult development to another, we are more able to put ourselves in others' shoes. Kegan's book *In Over Our Heads* is foundational to all things developmental, including leadership development.

Check out the work of system scientist and MIT professor Peter Senge, starting with *The Fifth Discipline* and *The Fifth Discipline Fieldbook*.

For more on systems read *Theory U: Leading from the Future as it Emerges* by C. Otto Scharmer.

Explore tough interpretations (Diagnose Situation) is a necessary prelude to test multiple interpretations. Testing interpretations (through observation, conversation and other modes of data collection) is the bridge from diagnosis to intervention.

Session ideas

1.

Create activities that allow people to walk in the shoes of other individuals or groups. For example, if you are developing leadership capacity in a system where there are competing factions (e.g., detained youth and corrections officers; gender-nonconforming youth who run away and do not feel safe in shelters structured for heterosexual youth, etc.), design activities that compel them to step into the role of someone with a competing perspective. The goal of the exercise is more than pure understanding. You are going for a mind shift but, more important, a heart shift.

2.

Begin your session design by making multiple, tough interpretations about the group you are serving. Consider yourself part of the system. Explore from every angle. See what ideas come to you when you start your session design process with diagnosis.

CHAPTER 4

Take the Temperature

Progress on adaptive challenges happens when you get the right people engaged and working toward a collective purpose. *Take the temperature,* a dimension of Diagnose Situation, means stopping to make sure you have enough of the right people engaged around a shared sense of purpose to make progress on your issue.

Your Leadership Edge p 36–41

We use metaphors like "level of heat," "hand on the thermostat" and "productive zone of work" to help learners visualize this aspect of Diagnose Situation. Basically, heat means discomfort. Progress on adaptive challenges requires people to be motivated by a sense of discomfort or dissatisfaction with the status quo.

Help those you teach and coach understand the need to constantly assess the temperature related to their adaptive challenge: How productively uncomfortable are people right now? This dimension is the diagnostic prelude to raising the heat skillfully and successfully. *Take the temperature* sets them up to keep a group collaborating long enough to make progress. It is not enough for people to leave your program ready to pump up the heat in a big attention-getting moment. They must also know how to maintain disciplined awareness of the fluctuations in the heat over time.

Design your leadership development programs to give people the opportunity to experience staying in diagnosis longer than they are used to and returning to diagnosis more often than feels natural. Reassure them with words like, "That's what it feels like to have your hand on the thermostat." Help them look inward as well to evaluate their own level of discomfort, or heat, related to an adaptive challenge. Provide experiences that allow them to understand the need to diagnose temperature at both the systemic and individual levels. Not everyone responds to a situation or intervention in the same way. So, unless you pay attention to individual reactions you run the risk of losing a key person as everyone else adjusts to a new reality.

As you teach, remember you, the leadership developer, are part of the system in your classroom: At any given moment is your own level of heat too high, too low or just right to be able to productively contribute to the success of the group?

Take the temperature is closely related to *raise the heat,* a dimension of Intervene Skillfully. Like *understand the process challenges* and *create a trustworthy process,* we often teach this Diagnose Situation/Intervene Skillfully pair together. We need to constantly attend to the temperature if we want to intervene successfully to keep people in the productive zone. Most often, the temperature is too low and we need to *raise the heat.* Other times, though, tempers flare and tensions rise requiring us to act to lower the heat. With a hand on the thermostat, we sense, and are ready to leverage, the moment when we get it right.

> **“Purpose matters. In coaching, I make a point of helping clients assess their own temperature relative to an issue. If the issue doesn’t matter enough to them, they will not do the work necessary to make progress.”**
>
> Howard Keim, PhD, ACC, KLC Coach

DEFINITIONS

Heat means discomfort. When facing an adaptive challenge, it is usually more comfortable for people to tolerate the status quo than risk the loss that may come with change. To spur people to do something different, we generate enough discomfort with the current reality that they feel compelled to change it.

Temperature is the level of heat or discomfort in a system or being experienced by an individual in relation to an adaptive challenge. If the level of heat is too low, the group or individual can avoid the work of creating change. If it is too high, interactions become unproductive, with too much conflict or people checked out completely. When the level of heat is just right, people find ways to collaborate on the challenge they face.

Productive zone is a visual metaphor (see page 191) for the optimal level of heat in a system to create real change. It describes a situation in which the right people are engaged around an adaptive challenge, with enough of a shared purpose that they feel compelled to experiment and, as a result, make progress.

Objectives

LEVEL 1

1. **Understand** *take the temperature* as necessary for good diagnosis and a step toward progress on adaptive challenges.

2. **See** that *take the temperature* and *raise the heat* are closely connected.

3. **Know** that while the heat is usually too low, it can sometimes get too high.

4. **Recognize** some verbal and nonverbal cues that indicate the temperature in the group.

5. **Know** we need to keep an eye on the temperature of individuals as well as the system.

6. **Stay** curious about the temperature in the system, especially when you feel uncertain about what to do next.

7. **Experience** the discomfort of staying in diagnosis longer than you are used to and returning to diagnosis more often than feels natural.

8. **Assess** and evaluate individual, internal level of heat, also known as productivity, related to an adaptive challenge. (Choose diagnostic moments. Consciously make observations and interpretations about your own actions and internal state. Get ready to use the data to drive interventions.)

9. **Assess** and evaluate the heat in the system, using data to determine your next move.

LEVEL 2

1. **Understand** that things we do to take the temperature (asking questions, silently observing, etc.) may also raise the heat.

2. **Know** that this aspect of diagnosis is useful in determining the ripeness of an issue.

3. **Trust** your hunches about the level of heat. (Sometimes the data is intangible. There's an energy shift. You just know.)

4. **Test** your hunches about the level of heat. (Sometimes your hunches are wrong.)

5. **Practice** taking the temperature constantly, amid the action. (Diagnose at multiple levels simultaneously: personal, between you and a partner, other people in the room, the group, larger context.)

6. **Take** the temperature to decide if it is the right time to attempt to make progress on something you care about.

7. **Facilitate** collective diagnosis of temperature. (Help a group get clear about the data they are using to diagnose ripeness, productivity, collective purpose and engagement of the right factions. Help others practice making observations that lead to interpretations about level of productivity.)

Q&A

Q: People engage in different ways and at different levels. In the classroom, how can I tell when the temperature is too cold or too hot?

A: If several people look bored, it is usually too cold. If several people seem to be working hard to keep emotions in check, it may be too hot. If you are unsure of the temperature, ask the group. Pause for a temperature check. Ask people where they would locate themselves relative to the productive zone. Answers will vary, but asking the question tends to raise the temperature and get more people paying attention to the work.

Q: When I'm teaching or facilitating, how can I get back on track when what's happening in the room is confusing or overwhelming (in other words, when the heat is too high within me)?

A: Slow yourself down by concentrating on your breathing for a few seconds. Make just one observation. Respond to one data point or comment at a time. Let the group help you sort it out. Remember, this is messy work. You won't do it perfectly. The group expects a non-anxious presence who keeps them moving, not someone who knows it all or rescues others.

In the real world

A resident of a tiny rural town has worried for years about the dilapidated, unoccupied and slowly melting house across the street. He sees the structure is a home for rats and stray cats and recognizes it as a danger to young children. However, the town council is reluctant to condemn the crumbling house, fearing to do so would set a precedent that could be used to limit private property rights in the future. The concerned resident runs for town council, wins and serves a full four-year term, listening, waiting, testing the waters with fellow council members, partnering on issues they care about, and biding time. Just after he is reelected for a second term, a near-tragedy happens when a 7-year-old girl in a neighboring community is trapped for several hours before being successfully rescued from a vacant building. The temperature around the issue of dangerous structures shoots up. Finally, the time is right and the council member makes the motion to condemn and tear down the melting house.

Resources

Your Leadership Edge, pages 36–41.

When Everyone Leads, *Part Four: Use the Heat.*

Cartoons – *Diagnose Situation Package*
go.kansasleadershipcenter.org/CT_DS

Teaching Leadership, page 171 and pages 173–176. Several of the coaching questions in this Manage Self section are useful in taking our own temperature and assessing our own tolerance of risk. The ideas on pages 152–154 apply to your presence when training and facilitating as well as coaching.

Emotional intelligence helps when taking the temperature. For inspiration and tools for working with yourself to prepare for engaging others in adaptive work, read *Compassionate Conversations: How to Speak and Listen from the Heart* by Diane Musho Hamilton, Gabriel Mengale Wilson and Kimberly Myosai Loh.

For more on emotional intelligence, check out these books:

- Richard Boyatzis and Annie McKee, *Resonant Leadership*, Harvard Business School Press, 2005.
- Daniel Goleman, *Emotional and Social Competency Inventory*, the Hay Group, 2007.
- Ellen Langer, *Mindfulness*, Merloyd Lawrence, 2014.

Capacity to take the temperature depends on the ability to manage triggers and navigate uncertainty and conflict (Manage Self). *Take the temperature* is an essential prelude to *raise the heat* (Intervene Skillfully). *Explore multiple interpretations* (Diagnose Situation) is closely connected as individuals' perceptions of the level of heat often differ.

Session ideas

1.

The productive zone chart on page 191, or a simple thermometer such as in the Diagnose Situation packet in the KLC store, helps people visualize taking the temperature. Test an interpretation about temperature with a question like: And what would we see that would let us know the heat is moving in the right direction for progress?

2.

If you want to teach *take the temperature* using a case from the real world, look for challenges related to transition planning and organizational change. Often someone in authority will fail to diagnose the readiness of others in the system before pushing a change forward.

CHAPTER 5

Identify Who Needs to Do the Work

Identify who needs to do the work is a dimension of Diagnose Situation and a bridge to the Energize Others dimensions _work across factions_ and _engage unusual voices_. As you teach this dimension, remind people that leadership on adaptive challenges is not about fixing the problem or controlling the situation.

Your Leadership Edge
p 42–49

Leadership is energizing and mobilizing others to create sustained positive change related to complex challenges. It is creating the conditions for the right people to step up, contribute and exercise leadership themselves. It is about finding ways for people who see the world from very different perspectives to navigate those differences and find a way forward that works.

As you teach this dimension, get people familiar with how we use terms like faction, values, loyalties, and losses. Encourage them to think about the word "identify" at two levels. At the first level, we identify the different factions who have something to contribute to a challenge. Then, we take the identifying a level deeper by getting curious about what members of each faction care about and what might keep them from exercising leadership and developing a shared sense of purpose.

To commit to this diagnostic behavior requires a determination to push beyond our blind spots. It can be hard, bias-confronting work to identify all the people who are impacted by a given issue or have an opinion about the best way forward. As we *identify who needs to do the work,* we also *explore multiple interpretations* about who needs to be involved in designing an engagement process. We force ourselves to identify all the factions who have a stake in the issue but whose perspectives on the problem might be difficult to deal with.

As we diagnose an adaptive challenge, we need to allow the experience of typically marginalized factions to inform the way people work together. We may need to practice radical empathy, for instance, when asking descendants of enslaved people to partner with predominantly white authority structures. Likewise, for persons of color, in many situations preparing to engage in adaptive work means tuning in to added dimensions of personal and profession risk, even while embracing the call to leadership.

It is essential that your students recognize that they are an integral part of any problem they seek to address. The person who wants to exercise leadership on an adaptive challenge is a member of a faction with its own values and loyalties. Have people practice naming the faction they represent and exploring their own values, loyalties, and potential losses in relation to the challenge. Provide space for them to make interpretations about how they may be impeding the progress they desire. Coach them to be honest about where they are willing to compromise. Coach them to assess their own loyalties, and reluctance to let go of the status quo. Encourage them to reflect in ways that help them empathize with the hard work they may be asking of others.

Part of teaching this dimension is helping people understand that they will not make progress on a complex challenge if they involve only the people they like, feel comfortable with, or typically bring to the table. Encourage them to practice making tough interpretations about their own role in silencing certain factions or keeping them from influencing outcomes. This leadership behavior, *identify who needs to do the work,* includes questioning who is being left behind, left out, kept out, ignored or marginalized.

> **“When coaching someone to identify who needs to do the work, help them consider that organizations often get stuck in a loop, with the same people doing the same work and wondering why nothing changes. Encourage your coachee to invite new voices into the conversation. New voices bring new, and often energizing, perspectives on the challenge.”**
>
> Thane Chastain, KLC Director of Virtual Learning and Engagement

DEFINITIONS

Faction is a group of people who share common values, are loyal to the same things and share a common orientation to the work. It is most effective, when attempting to exercise leadership, to describe a faction other than your own in noble terms, as they might describe themselves.

Values are deeply held beliefs related to an adaptive challenge, often based on significant life experience, and revealed through actions and behaviors.

Loyalties describe dedication to a group, place, people or way of doing things that may become barriers to progress on the adaptive challenge at hand. Loyalties often trump values.

Losses are what a faction gives up if progress is made on an adaptive challenge. For example, control, security, prestige, familiarity, etc. People anticipate losses and see risks they are not willing to take.

Objectives

LEVEL 1

1. **Understand** that adaptive work cannot be accomplished by you alone, or by an expert or person in authority alone. Stakeholders in multiple factions need to be engaged.

2. **Understand** that the work involves identifying multiple stakeholders who must be mobilized to exercise leadership.

3. **Know** the definitions of faction, values, loyalties, and losses.

4. **Know** that part of the process of identifying who needs to do the work is understanding who the factions are and what they value, are loyal to, and stand to lose if progress happens.

5. **Feel** implicated by the idea that even the person who seeks to exercise leadership is part of the system that created the problem. (Realize, "I am part of the mess.")

6. **Notice** what it feels like to understand that, with adaptive work, there are multiple stakeholders who must do the work. (Is it liberating for you? Scary because you must cede control? Etc.?)

7. **List** the individuals and factions who may need to do the work. (Make a faction map.)

8. **Make** interpretations about each faction's values, loyalties and potential losses, and how important it is to engage them in making progress.

9. **Choose** who is essential to making progress.

LEVEL 2

1. **Recognize** that with adaptive work the people with the problem (maybe the people your organization serves) have an essential role to play in making progress.

2. **Practice** imagining the barriers to engagement and leadership that exist for the people who need to do the work.

3. **Explore** the context surrounding an adaptive challenge and understand the structures and processes that may create barriers to engagement and leave some people behind.

4. **Make** and test interpretations about what it will take to give the work back to the people who need to do the work.

Q&A

Q: How do you keep people from getting overwhelmed with all the moving parts associated with multiple stakeholders?

A: Offer tools they can use, like KLC's faction map, so they can get past the ambiguity and begin to see the value of a thorough diagnostic process. Encourage them to start small. For instance, have one exploratory conversation with a representative of a faction they normally wouldn't engage with.

In the real world

Listen to Chana Joffe-Walt's podcast *Nice White Parents,* for an example of an adaptive challenge that involved multiple factions organizing against racial segregation in New York public schools, with mixed results: www.thisamericanlife.org/712/nice-white-parents. Who needs to be energized to do the work to make more progress—and eventually solve—this important challenge? Who are the individuals and factions who could exercise leadership within their spheres of influence?

Resources

Your Leadership Edge, pages 42–49.

When Everyone Leads, Chapter 16, *Start Engaging Others.*

KLC Guidebook, pages 30–31.

Cartoons – Diagnose Situation Package
go.kansasleadershipcenter.org/CT_DS

Video – Who's Not at the Table
go.kansasleadershipcenter.org/Table

Video – Your Part of the Mess
go.kansasleadershipcenter.org/Mess

Part of *identifying who needs to do the work* (Diagnose Situation) is *exploring tough interpretations* (Diagnose Situation) about who has not yet been engaged and why. And once you've identified your factions, you'll need to find ways to *test multiple interpretations* (Diagnose Situation) about how to work with them. When you are ready to move beyond testing, it's time to *give the work back* (Intervene Skillfully) and *work across factions* (Energize Others). Prepare to *manage vulnerabilities and triggers* (Manage Self) associated with giving up control. When the work is adaptive, you cannot do it alone.

Watch Eric Lui's TED Talk: *Why Ordinary People Need to Understand Power*

For helpful inspiration when trying to identify factions and who needs to do the work check out research by the Center for Creative Leadership on what they call Boundary Spanning Leadership.

Session ideas

1.

Home for the Hawksbill is a beautifully shot 30 minute video (available on YouTube) documenting The Nature Conservancy's work to engage people across complicated tribal and cultural divides to save the dwindling population of the Hawksbill Sea Turtle in the South Pacific country of the Solomon Islands. Show the video. Then have participants identify factions, their values, and what each risked in engaging with the others.

2.

Use a current, real-life challenge that everyone has some stake in (such as working virtually during a pandemic). Ask people to identify the factions and use those that emerge to discuss what it means to determine who needs to do the work.

CHAPTER 6

Test Multiple Interpretations

"Next!"

In the 2010 version of our leadership framework the wording of this dimension was "test multiple interpretations and points of view." Rewritten in 2020 to focus on testing the validity and usefulness of an interpretation, we see *test multiple interpretations* as a bridge between the competency of Diagnose Situation and the more action-oriented competencies of Intervene Skillfully, Energize Others and even Manage Self.

Your Leadership Edge
p 50-55

• • • • •

Test multiple interpretations must be paired but never conflated with *explore tough interpretations,* another dimension of Diagnose Situation. Only after we've explored a wide range of interpretations are we equipped to decide which are worth testing. Because we haven't written much about this anywhere else, we'll briefly expand on the distinctions between the two dimensions here.

Explore tough interpretations describes the act of imagining as many perspectives and ways to make meaning of a situation as possible. The word "tough" as part of this dimension reminds us to push ourselves to consider interpretations that are systemic, "tough-on-me" and indicative that the work required is adaptive, rather than technical.

Test multiple interpretations directs us to take two further action steps. First, choose the most compelling interpretations. Second, implement tests designed to get to know those interpretations better and understand how important and valid they may be. *Test multiple interpretations* implies action, but it cautions against jumping right to a full-scale intervention. It also cautions against getting stuck on just one interpretation. *Interpretations* in this dimension is plural, meaning test more than one explanation of what could be going on.

A test could mean more observation and more conversation, seeking data to determine how valid, true or important the interpretation is. Testing an interpretation involves gathering clues about how likely it is that further action and experiments based on the interpretation will lead to important learning and progress. Only after you've tested more than one interpretation should you move to more high-risk experimentation.

We use the Observe-Interpret-Intervene (O-I-I) cycle, shown at the top of page 71, to help learners visualize the iterative process of making and testing interpretations before moving to interventions, which may involve significant risk to self or system. At the top of the cycle, we observe from multiple perspectives. Then we interpret; we explore tough interpretations. *Test multiple interpretations* is the part of the cycle bridging Interpret and Intervene. When we test an interpretation, we have one foot in the competency of Diagnose Situation and another in the more action-oriented competencies of Intervene Skillfully, Energize Others or Manage Self.

"The quality of your tests depends on first engaging a broad range of voices in generating tough, systemic interpretations. Without the genius of everyone involved, the outcome may not be successful, no matter how many tests you conduct."

Mildred Edwards, PhD, ACC, KLC Coach

Make Tough Interpretations

Easy-On-Me:
Interpretations that don't challenge the status quo or the story we like to tell.

Tough-On-Me:
Raises the heat by revealing unspoken motivations and "our part of the mess."

Individual:
Accounting for actions by assigning cause to a specific individual.

Systemic:
Accounts for pressures, patterns and roles that exist in any group.

Objectives

LEVEL 1

1. **Understand** the distinction between *explore tough interpretations* and *test multiple interpretations.*

2. **Understand** how *explore* and *test* fit within the Observe-Interpret-Intervene cycle.

3. **Know** that because progress on adaptive challenges requires everyone in a system to learn, change and tolerate losses, leadership typically requires us to test interpretations that don't match with our own worldview or preferences.

4. **Practice** multiple ways of testing an interpretation

LEVEL 2

1. **Understand** that not all interpretations are worth testing.

2. **Coach** self and others to determine which interpretations are worth investing the time to test.

3. **Design** tests with proper scope and level of risk to self and system. (The scope is too big if you don't have access to the information you need to implement or evaluate the test. The risk is too high if one possible outcome of the test would eliminate your future capacity to intervene on the issue or if it would put important aspects of your organization in danger.)

4. **Link** each test backward to an interpretation and forward to what we expect to learn.

5. **Test** multiple interpretations related to a challenge.

In the real world

Five people are charged with planning a conference for their national professional association. One person has come up with a theme and the rest start recommending topics. Midway through their first meeting, however, they catch themselves and realize they need to test their interpretations about the needs of the association members. They survey the field and what they learn reveals the distance between their nascent plans and others' aspirations for a successful event. They switch gears and design a more informed intervention. The conference is well-attended and helps take the association to new levels of opportunity for impact in their field.

Staff members of an organization trying to become more equitable and inclusive have formal and informal conversations with the stakeholders they seek to engage. The goal is to test their interpretations of what would make their services more welcoming and useful to people of color and people with disabilities who typically stay away.

Q&A

Q: What is the difference between *exploring* interpretations and *testing* them?

A: Both are leadership behaviors associated with Diagnose Situation. When we say *explore tough interpretations* we mean make lists of all possible interpretations. List easy-to-address and difficult-to-stomach explanations for what's going on in your leadership challenge. Look at the situation from all angles and take educated guesses. Be brave enough to push beyond your first idea. Then make some choices. Set your wildest and simplest interpretations aside in favor of just two or three that seem worth testing. Ideate and explore first. Then test.

Resources

Your Leadership Edge, pages 50–55.

KLC Guidebook, pages 16 and 17.

Cartoons – Diagnose Situation Package
go.kansasleadershipcenter.org/CT_DS

Listen to Nigerian author Chimamanda Ngozi-Adichie as she reflects on the danger of a single story:
go.kansasleadershipcenter.org/Chimamanda

Human centered design methods force a team to prototype an idea as a test with the focus on learning versus success. One resource is www.designkit.org/methods

Test multiple interpretations (Diagnose Situation) overlaps with *act experimentally* (Intervene Skillfully). The emphasis may be slightly more on learning in the former, while the latter is an informed attempt at making progress.

Session ideas

Work with participants to create a faction map to identify diverse perspectives and explore possible interpretations about a challenge. Then, have them test the validity of those interpretations in cross-faction conversations. Work with them to design a low risk experiment to further test the points of view elevated in the map. Finally, coach them to update their interpretations and use only those that have passed the tests as the jumping-off points for higher-risk experiments.

PART TWO

MANAGE SELF

Those who aspire to exercise more leadership need to know themselves well enough to choose when and how to intervene.

Design programs to help people prepare to manage themselves. Provide time for them to reflect and identify their vulnerabilities and triggers, the hot buttons others can press to take them out of the game. They'll need to know the story others tell about them. They'll need to choose among competing values. Make time for them to explore the values and habits that have held them back from intervening in the past, the risks they have been unwilling to take to make progress on something they care about.

Prepare them to tolerate uncertainty and conflict. Create opportunities for them to practice doing what is needed, not what is comfortable. Exercising leadership on tough challenges will require them to get out of their comfort zones.

Finally, they can't manage themselves, let alone exercise leadership, without taking care of themselves. Burnout is not a leadership behavior. Help them prioritize self-care—physical, emotional, spiritual, intellectual—so they are ready to seize opportunities to lead.

CHAPTER 7

Manage Your Vulnerabilities and Triggers

As we turn to the competency Manage Self and the dimension *manage your vulnerabilities and triggers,* it is helpful to reorient to the principle that *leadership starts with you and must engage others.* Managing oneself is the hardest part of exercising leadership. At the same time, managing oneself well is not enough. We manage ourselves so we can be poised to diagnose situations, energize other people, and intervene to skillfully address complex challenges.

Your Leadership Edge p 58–65

KLC's 2020 curriculum review brought a rewrite to this first dimension of Manage Self. Formerly *know your strengths, vulnerabilities and triggers,* our team decided to focus on vulnerabilities and triggers since those are what tend to get people in trouble. More important, we want to emphasize that knowing or being aware of your vulnerabilities and triggers is never enough. To effectively mobilize others to do difficult, adaptive work we must take steps to proactively manage our vulnerabilities and triggers. We refer to this dimension now as *manage your vulnerabilities and triggers.*

As you teach this dimension, give people plenty of time to grapple with the definitions of vulnerabilities and triggers and practice identifying examples of their own. Share instances when your own vulnerabilities adversely affected your ability to lead. Tell a self-deprecating story of a time you were triggered and describe what might have gone differently if you'd managed the trigger better. Help students see, from their own experience, how triggers and vulnerabilities show up differently depending on the challenge, situation, people they need to work with, and type of leadership required. Provide space for people to reflect on a current adaptive challenge that is important to them. Have them name the factions involved and consider triggers that might arise as they attempt to engage with members of each.

Give people a chance to talk about and understand for themselves why *manage your vulnerabilities and triggers* is a leadership behavior. Make it personal by asking: What makes this dimension hard for you? What might become possible if you managed your triggers more often and effectively? Encourage people to share ideas and embrace new habits for becoming both more mindful about their vulnerabilities and triggers and better equipped to manage them when they arise.

If managing oneself were easy we'd all make more progress on our adaptive challenges. Like every other dimension of leadership covered in *Your Leadership Edge,* this one is most difficult to do when we most need to do it. Motivate people in their efforts to manage vulnerabilities and triggers differently by linking the work back to purpose. Remind them: Leadership is not about you and all the reasons you are justified in being triggered or annoyed. It is about prioritizing self-management for the sake of making progress on something important to you and those you care about most.

> **"No matter how much authority I have, or you have, we won't be able to energize others or intervene skillfully if we can't manage ourselves. With any adaptive challenge there will be internal factions characterized by divergent values. They will trigger each other. I can't let that reality frustrate me or trigger me. If I know my values, and anticipate and manage my triggers, I can effectively navigate, and hopefully unite, the factions to make progress on our challenge."**
>
> Jonathan McRoy, KLC Associate

DEFINITIONS

Vulnerabilities can be anything that leaves you open to attack and diminishes your capacity to lead effectively. For instance, they may be secrets, difficult relationships, past mistakes, private ambitions or personal cravings that could limit your ability to lead. Implicit biases are vulnerabilities until we make them conscious and consider how they affect our diagnosis. Sometimes your role is a vulnerability. An unmanaged trigger is a vulnerability.

Triggers are actions, behaviors, events or ideas that simply set you off, negatively or positively, and cause you to react in a manner that interferes with relationships, performance, values, and goals. If someone or something threatens to exploit one of your vulnerabilities, that someone or something may become a trigger.

Objectives

LEVEL 1

1. **Understand** the definitions of vulnerabilities and triggers, and how they are related.
2. **Know** why managing vulnerabilities and triggers is a leadership behavior.
3. **Identify** personal triggers and vulnerabilities and how they interfere with the work of leadership.
4. **Reflect** on past behavior and notice in the here-and-now how you typically respond to a trigger or work to cover up a vulnerability.
5. **Learn** and practice simple mindfulness habits for noticing and responding to a trigger in a productive manner.

LEVEL 2

1. **Understand** the relationship between managing your vulnerabilities and triggers and your ability to consciously, skillfully intervene.
2. **Experience** insight about how a personal trigger connects to a value or experience and how exploring the link to a value or life experience makes the trigger or vulnerability more manageable.
3. **Prioritize** progress on adaptive challenges over indulging a trigger or vulnerability.
4. **Practice** managing vulnerabilities and triggers effectively in situations that require leadership.

In the real world

With the dimensions of Manage Self, including manage your vulnerabilities and triggers, you have countless examples to draw on from your own life. Share your stories, struggles and successes with those you seek to develop. Let them know that even "experts" aren't done learning and practicing the leadership art of self-management. What vulnerabilities have you learned to negotiate? What is your go-to, in-the-moment method for managing a trigger? When has it failed you?

Self-management is nowhere more important than in efforts to build understanding, and change behavior through diversity, equity, and inclusion work. Managing our triggers means practicing empathy, acknowledging trauma, and recognizing our own privilege. Others' perspectives and interpretations may run counter to memories of our childhoods and things we've experienced as true about ourselves, setting us up to be triggered. Consider your triggers and vulnerabilities related to complicated intersections of race, class, and economic impoverishment.

Q&A

Q: Is it fair to promise people that this behavior gets easier with age?

A: No. This behavior gets easier with practice. To get better at this aspect of self-management, you'll need practices to make you aware of vulnerabilities and triggers before they impede your exercise of leadership. You'll also need to practice replacing your typical triggered reaction with a considered, purposeful response.

Resources

Your Leadership Edge, pages 58–64.

When Everyone Leads, *Part Three: Start With You.*

Cartoons – Manage Self Package
go.kansasleadershipcenter.org/CT_MS

Worksheets – Manage Self Package
go.kansasleadershipcenter.org/WS_MS

Video – What's Your Part of the Mess
go.kansasleadershipcenter.org/Mess

KLC Guidebook, pages 36–37.

Brené Brown writes about "the hustle for worthiness." When you are doing the hustle, instead of finding ways to deal directly or openly with limitations you expend energy hiding these vulnerable parts of yourself. You play it safe or overcompensate. Sometimes your unwillingness to be vulnerable can be the ultimate vulnerability. See Brené Brown's famous TED Talk, *The Power of Vulnerability*.

Practices such as mindfulness and yoga help build awareness of and ability to manage triggers. Check out Jon Kabat-Zinn's book *Mindfulness for Beginners*.

Short, free, online yoga at yogadownload.com.

Leadership starts with you and must engage others is a leadership principle, and it's hard, if not impossible, to start anything significant or engage anyone in a meaningful way if you are triggered or hustling to hide a vulnerability.

Session ideas

1.

Have individuals reflect on a trigger or triggering event and journal about the experience. Provide prompts such as: Did it involve one of my core values? Did this have something to do with how I feel about a past similar event? What happens if I let it impact my performance and goals? What is a possible way to manage myself through this trigger?

2.

Create a worksheet or classroom activity to invite students to practice moving from knowing to managing triggers. Prompts could include: Make a list of your known triggers. Brainstorm ways to manage them in the weeks to come. Choose and talk with an accountability partner. Plan to check in with your partner.

CHAPTER 8

Get Used to Uncertainty and Conflict

Uncertainty and conflict are markers of 21st century life. Those who want to exercise leadership more effectively need you, the leadership developer, to create environments that compel them to practice this dimension of Manage Self.

Your Leadership Edge
p 66–71

Get used to uncertainty and conflict is unique among among dimensions of the leadership competencies in that it is wholly internal work. It represents the process of insight, reflection and will-building required to do things like *work across factions* and *experiment beyond your comfort zone.*

Though the work is internal, it is difficult for students to do the necessary reflection unless we compel them to enter situations where they experience uncertainty and conflict and feel their uncomfortable effects. Getting used to uncertainty requires living through the muscle tension, pounding heart, flushed cheeks and shallow breathing that comes with putting ourselves in unpleasant and unfamiliar situations.

We rarely dedicate a separate session to teaching this idea. Rather, we weave the objectives listed in this chapter among other sessions and activities. Anything you design that encourages people to speak up with a provocative question, propose a contradictory interpretation, or intervene when they are unsure of what the result will be is an exercise in getting used to uncertainty and conflict. So, find a time to introduce the behavior or refer to it as a key element of the leadership competency Manage Self, but let people learn it as they attempt to intervene or as you debrief work related to another dimension. Use questions like: What was it like to make that tough interpretation? And what did you experience in your body as you made that attempt at speaking to loss?

Another way to help people *get used to uncertainty and conflict* is to encourage them to speak up in your classrooms in ways they are not prepared to in the world outside. Remind them that by speaking up, for instance, about a pattern of discrimination they are seizing an opportunity to *get used to uncertainty and conflict* that will prepare them to manage themselves more effectively in other situations.

When we, as leadership developers, coach people to pause, reflect and celebrate that they did something hard and learned something useful as a result, we help them build their *get used to uncertainty and conflict* muscle. We can draw attention to what they did, prompt them to notice how they experienced it internally, and celebrate the fact that they did not die as a result. The hope is, next time, they will step into uncertainty or conflict with a little less hesitation, a more reasonable assessment of the personal risk involved, and a greater willingness to experience a rising heart rate or queasy stomach for the sake of something bigger than themselves. Progress on entrenched and complex challenges does not happen without conflict. When the work is adaptive there will be competing perspectives to work through. Those we teach must be willing to go there.

DEFINITIONS

Values are beliefs (conscious and unconscious, noble and less noble) that drive attitudes, choices and behaviors. Values are revealed through actions and behaviors.

> **"The COVID-19 pandemic created a great and intense level of uncertainty and conflict for all my clients, personally and professionally. Having my clients take a step back and examine their vulnerabilities and triggers, along with their strengths, helped them to identify what was most challenging for them about the situation. They also got clarity about internal resources to not only cope but lead and make progress during the pandemic."**
>
> **Phyllis Collins, ACC, KLC Coach**

Objectives

LEVEL 1

1. **Understand** that conflict is a normal and necessary ingredient for progress.

2. **Notice** what uncertainty feels like physiologically. Practice becoming aware of and tolerating the signals.

3. **Examine** tough (uncertain, conflicted) moments from the past as a way of building capacity to manage oneself through uncertainty and conflict in the present and future.

4. **Identify** moments of uncertainty as they happen (in the classroom and back at home).

5. **Identify** moments of opportunity to choose to turn toward or away from conflict (in the classroom and back at home).

6. **Recognize** that the clearer and more important the purpose, the more willing we are to tolerate uncertainty and conflict.

LEVEL 2

1. **Intervene** differently in moments of uncertainty or conflict, resisting temptation to lower the heat.

2. **Experience** intervening differently in tense moments as one way of building capacity to tolerate uncertainty and conflict in the future.

3. **Build** tolerance for tough conversations and systemic interpretations related to difficult topics.

In the real world

Don't expect to will away discomfort. Instead, practice living with it. In the 1960s, civil rights activists prepared for lunch counter sit-ins with training in how to resist striking back at aggressors. To prepare young African Americans for the sit-ins, the NAACP ran an experiential course known as "Social Drama." Would-be nonviolent protesters subjected themselves to abuse including smoke in the face, hair pulling, coffee spilling and being hit with a newspaper. Only those who remained calm during training graduated to the more intense uncertainty and conflict of restaurant lunch counters.

Q&A

Q: How do I know if people are building tolerance for uncertainty and conflict?

A: Your students will speak up, act, intervene more often once they accept that the only way to find out what is going to happen is, in fact, to do something and see what happens. When that "this could work; let's see what happens" attitude shows up in your classroom it means someone is getting used to stepping into uncertainty and, potentially, conflict, which often takes the form of someone naming the elephant in the room.

Resources

Your Leadership Edge, pages 66–71.

Teaching Leadership: Case-in-Point, Case Studies and Coaching, Session 5 – *Manage Self: Know your Strengths, Vulnerabilities and Triggers,* pp. 216–218; Session 6 – *Manage Self: Experiment Beyond Your Comfort Zone,* pp 219–223.

Cartoons – Manage Self Package
go.kansasleadershipcenter.org/CT_MS

Worksheets – Manage Self Package
go.kansasleadershipcenter.org/WS_MS

Video – Uncertainty and Conflict
go.kansasleadershipcenter.org/UandC

For training and experience in conflict resolution and mediation, and to build capacity to tolerate conflict, check out www.ccrchicago.org/training-programs and go.kansasleadershipcenter.org/cr

When leading through change, it is necessary to help others cope with change. Check out William Bridges' book *Transitions: Making Sense of Life's Changes*, revised edition 2019. Or learn about the Bridges Transition Model at wmbridges.com/about/what-is-transition

Check out psychologist Ryan Howe's blog on How to Confront at go.kansasleadershipcenter.org/HtC

Learning for Justice is a program of the Southern Poverty Law Center, based in Montgomery, Alabama. It offers resources to use when the conflict and uncertainty centers around racial equity. See www.learningforjustice.org

Session ideas

1.

Worksheets and coaching questions related to *act experimentally* (Intervene Skillfully) are useful for this dimension of Manage Self, too. The concept of experimenting is new to many people. Uncertainty, a sense of incompetence or unpreparedness, and all the unknowns related to an adaptive challenge are part and parcel of each experiment. Encourage someone to experiment and they'll have to practice getting used to uncertainty and conflict.

2.

Watch this video of young people engaging in tense dialogue about the legacy of slavery in their own lives. Pause the video two or three times and ask class members to check in with their feelings and sensations. Have them reflect in writing: What are you experiencing in your body? How would you manage the uncertainty and respond productively in a moment like this?
www.nationalgeographic.org/media/american-textures

3.

Draw on activities from the field of conflict management and resolution.

4.

Show Brook Detterline's TEDx Talk, *Creating Ethical Culture in Business* and facilitate a discussion of what it feels like to choose in the moment to elevate doing the right thing over maintaining the status quo of comfortable relationships.

CHAPTER 9

Choose Among Competing Values

As you set out to teach *choose among competing values,* remember, this dimension exists within the competency of Manage Self. It focuses on hard choices you must make about how to use your time, talent, life energy and social capital. It compels you to decide what matters most, set a few firm priorities and open yourself to compromise on almost everything else. It encourages you to make the risky choice to exercise leadership.

Your Leadership Edge
p 72-79

It is easy, when introducing this dimension, to slide into conversation about an organization's competing values. Save that for your Diagnose Situations sessions on *explore tough interpretations.* Keep this work focused on self-management and hard individual choices.

Choose among competing values highlights the grim reality that most of us avoid acts of leadership most of the time. Most of us regularly (if unthinkingly) choose comfort over risk, predictability over progress, status over impact, our own preferences over the good of the group, complacency over leadership. We build our to-do lists and check items off one by one. We revel in efficiency and expertise. Busyness is our excuse for avoiding adaptive work.

Importantly, this dimension calls for your students and coaching clients to make their values choices consciously. According to Marty Linsky, making progress on the big issues that divide our families, communities and country requires compromising, prioritizing and honoring the values of other people, sometimes over your own. Linsky gives hints about how to teach this dimension of Manage Self. Encourage students who want to contribute to progress on adaptive challenges to "do the painful work of ordering your priorities and focusing only on what is at or near to the top of your list." As a leadership developer, you can empathize with people's desire to prioritize everything. Coach them to pick the things they value most and be willing to compromise on everything else.

One way to think about this dimension is as a choice between leadership and comfort. Push your students to answer for themselves: What do I value so much that I am willing to risk my own comfort to exercise leadership?

Treat *choose among competing values* as a Manage Self behavior and help those you teach explore whether they have been unconsciously using values like busyness, comfort, complacency, and unwillingness to compromise as excuses for not taking action. Often values are unconscious and the first step in managing ourselves is noticing what we've been prioritizing. Once we've admitted, for instance, that we have been valuing looking busy over making progress on something we care about, we have the opportunity to choose our own, more conscious, way forward.

Another nuance of *choose among competing values* is that sometimes, to make progress, we need to compromise and elevate someone else's values over our own. All the more reason to know the difference between our top two or three values, and those that may be negotiable.

"Black, Indigenous and People of Color (BIPOC) often report feeling required to choose among competing values in the workforce and other arenas in which they are not the majority. Fear of isolation or loss fuels day-to-day interactions and causes them to manage themselves in ways they perceive are expected to retain employment. Difficult internal work in a coaching relationship may be best focused on refining their authentic voice and using it to effectively impact the systems they navigate."

Mildred Edwards, PHD, ACC, KLC Coach,

DEFINITIONS

Values are beliefs (conscious and unconscious, noble and less noble) that drive attitudes, choices and behaviors. Values are revealed through actions and behaviors.

> **"There will be a point, when you are at the front of the room, when you have to choose between the value of providing what participants want (usually order, protection or direction) and what may be best for their learning (uncertainty, heat, elevating conflict). When you name these values, contradictions and the choices available to you in the moment, you take a great opportunity to allow the group to examine how competing values impact our leadership."**
>
> Patrick Kelly, KLC Teacher and Civic Facilitator

Objectives

LEVEL 1

1. **Define** values in this context.
2. **Understand** that values compete for attention in our lives.
3. **Recognize** that by failing to consciously choose to exercise leadership we are choosing the status quo.
4. **Learn** that sometimes unconscious values drive us.
5. **Sit** with the discomfort of internal tug of war between competing values.

LEVEL 2

1. **Choose** between competing values when working on an adaptive challenge.
2. **Recognize** that other people have deeply held values and to make progress we may have to elevate one of their values over our own.
3. **Understand** how systemic pressures dictate individual values.
4. **Experience** the complex layers of competing values around a challenge, and how reconciling them requires difficult internal work.

In the real world

You might recall a time when you rebelled against the values instilled by your family. Choosing our own core values is key to adult development. As we grow older, we abandon some values while strengthening our commitment to others. Leadership moments that require us to choose one value over another may end up shaping our identity.

For many white Americans, contributing to a racially equitable culture in an organization or community means choosing to elevate new, more inclusive practices over the benefits and security of the status quo.

Q&A

Q: I've tried to help people learn what's stated in Level 2, Objective 2, "Recognize that other people have deeply held values and to make progress we may have to elevate one of their values over our own." But I find many people see it as a matter of principle that they stick to their values no matter what. How can I get them to open their minds?

A: This is a Level 2 objective for a reason. You can't push another person along their developmental path. Work with them on choosing between two of their own values first (the Level 1 objectives). Trust that life will be their teacher.

Resources

Your Leadership Edge, pages 72–79.

When Everyone Leads, Chaper 8, *Values Clash When You Seek to Close the Gap*, provides a systemic take on this idea.

Cartoons – Manage Self Package
go.kansasleadershipcenter.org/CT_MS

Worksheets – Manage Self Package
go.kansasleadershipcenter.org/WS_MS

Choosing among competing values may be difficult because we think we can quantify those values. In Ruth Chang's TED talk, *How to Make Hard Choices,* she argues that in making hard choices, we uncover something about ourselves, elevating our values and creating our own identities. Check it out at go.kansasleadershipcenter.org/choices

Check out this article written by Nate Boyer in which he reckons with the competing values of patriotism and protesting at go.kansasleadershipcenter.org/NateBoyer

Bottom line: Almost every act of leadership described in the *Your Leadership Edge* requires a choice between competing values. The essential question is: What do I care about enough to risk exercising leadership? Some values, too, are unconscious. It's good practice to *explore tough interpretations* (Diagnose Situation) of how our unconscious values impact our work. Failure to choose among competing values makes a person vulnerable to being pulled off track by another person with a strong point of view or sense of purpose. So, *choose among competing values* (Manage Self), *know the stories others tell about you* (Manage Self), and *manage your vulnerabilities and triggers* often need be practiced together.

Session ideas

Have program participants (or coaching clients) log their activities for two weeks in half-hour increments. At the end of the two weeks they reflect upon the list. Each person asks themselves: What do these activities say about my values? Do my activities reflect my espoused values? Do my activities demonstrate leadership on behalf of something I care about? What semi-conscious values have been elevated in this log? What tough choices do I need to make?

CHAPTER 10

Know the Stories Others Tell About You

Developing leadership capacity in others means helping them discern what stories to pay attention to and how to use those stories to support effective interventions. Each person has a range of possible roles they can play, moves they can make, and approaches they can take in situations requiring leadership. If a challenge is adaptive, a person who seeks to exercise leadership needs to meet other people where they are and energize them to play their part in creating change. *Know the stories others tell about you* is like sticking a toe in the ocean. Icy cold or bathtub warm doesn't have to change your plan to get in the water, but it might make a difference in how fast you go.

Your Leadership Edge
p 80–85

We have made a small but meaningful rewrite to this dimension of Manage Self. Formerly *know the story others tell about you,* we now use the plural, "stories." It's important to remind anyone who wants to exercise leadership that there are as many stories about our strengths, weaknesses, roles, relationships and approaches to leadership as there are people in our orbit to come up with them.

The ideas in *Your Leadership Edge,* and especially the competency Manage Self, assumes that I am part of any system I seek to change. Teach people to turn a curious eye on themselves as they work on a challenge, or simply interact in the classroom around the shared challenge of learning and practicing leadership skills. Coach them to reflect on questions like: How are individuals or the group I want to energize reacting to me? Do they build on my comments and questions? Are there any patterns in how they respond to me? Do things change depending on who else is in the room? Given my level of authority, might they be keeping anything from me? What do they seem to depend on me for? What happens when I disappoint expectations? What do I represent for this person or that person? Do any of the stories have more to do with my role than with my behavior? Are my interventions having the impact I intend?

Meanwhile, encourage people to look inward for stories too. Coach them to identify any pressure they feel to behave in certain ways. Have them explore the expectations the system has for them, and what might be gained (or risked) if they showed up differently. Help people understand that *know the stories others tell about you* doesn't require them to change anything if they don't want to. It simply reveals what is already there and allows them to make more informed choices about how they intervene.

> **"Paying attention to know the stories others tell about you does not mean being overly sensitive about what others think. It does not mean you need to change in response to every bit of feedback you receive. This behavior is about collecting the data you need to deploy yourself in more effective ways with those you intend to mobilize."**
>
> Kevin Bomhoff, ACC, KLC Senior Associate

Objectives

LEVEL 1

1. **Understand** why knowing the stories is a necessary aspect of managing self and an important developmental opportunity if you want to exercise leadership more effectively.

2. **Consider** how people typically perceive you, how that is different than your own perceptions, when it is useful to live up to those stories, and when it might not be.

3. **Experience** a sense of curiosity and opportunity (rather than defensiveness) when asked to acknowledge the importance of looking at self through the eyes of others.

4. **Entertain** ways in which those who wish you well would encourage you to grow and develop.

5. **Identify** specific steps to gather feedback when you go back home.

LEVEL 2

1. **Identify** patterns among stories told about you.

2. **Explore** systemic pressures that support your own default behaviors.

3. **Distinguish** stories about yourself from stories about your role(s).

4. **Clarify** which stories empower and which inhibit you.

5. **Consider** ways to leverage prevailing stories for a purpose.

Q&A

Q: Students and coaching clients constantly ask, "How do I find out how others really perceive me?" What should I tell them?

A: Sometimes things are as simple and as uncomfortable as they seem at first glance. The short answer is, if you want to know what another person thinks about you, ask them. Additional advice could be, make sure they trust you enough to give you the truth. And be prepared to hear it. If they are not willing to state the truth, that is an opportunity to get curious with them to understand why. Another approach is to get curious about how people respond to your attempts at leadership. Watch what they do and say in response to your interventions. Then, work backward to imagine what story might cause them to react that way. Finally, consider the possibility that they are already trying to tell you, and you are just not listening. If you ever feel defensive, that's data.

In the real world

A KLC alum served on a high-level telecommunications advisory committee, representing the point of view of city administrators and local elected officials. The committee was dominated by people from the telecommunications industry whose prevailing view of city government was negative. The KLC-trained city official worked hard to understand the pressures facing telecom industry representatives as they build infrastructure to serve a community. He consistently applied the ideas from *Your Leadership Edge* in hopes of creating focus on a common purpose, and space for understanding differences. As the work progressed, colleagues on the committee remarked that the KLC alum's purposeful approach caused them to be more open to his thoughts and ideas, and more willing to care about challenges facing cities when working with telecom companies. Midway through the work, the chairman took our friend aside, saying, "I don't know what you did, but we have never seen this kind of cooperation and progress between the industry and cities." That unsolicited feedback told the KLC alum he was on the right track. One of the stories people were telling about him was that his interventions were helping the group find common ground.

Resources

Your Leadership Edge, pages 80–85.

When Everyone Leads, Chapter 15, *Start With Your Part of the Mess.*

Cartoons – Manage Self Package
go.kansasleadershipcenter.org/CT_MS

Worksheets – Manage Self Package
go.kansasleadershipcenter.org/WS_MS

Assessments such as the Kolbe Learning Style Inventory and the Myers-Briggs Type Indicator help you see yourself through the eyes of coworkers whose learning and relating styles are different from your own.

This dimension of Manage Self informs what you do to *inspire a collective purpose* (Energize Others). As you understand others' stories about you, you get clues about how you may need to change your behavior to successfully engage them toward a common purpose.

Session ideas

1.

Create a worksheet to support creative application of this dimension. Include prompts like "The stories others tell about me are a suit of armor when..., a burden when..., a compass when..., clothes that no longer fit me when..., ammunition when..."

2.

Learn from the fields of branding, marketing and politics. Create a fun activity in which participants research their existing brand and design a website or flyer to build a stronger, more purposeful one.

3.

Pause during a class session and demonstrate this dimension in action by musing out loud about the stories people in the room might be telling about you, the instructor. After you've shared a few possibilities (and invited people to give you their own insights) have a discussion about how you might use those stories as hints about how to adjust your teaching, and about how this aspect of Manage Self could help you be more effective.

CHAPTER 11

Experiment Beyond Your Comfort Zone

"Yeah, I get the part about you feeling better with training wheels on, but here's the thing..."

When you seek to develop leadership capacity in others, make sure they get this message: Nothing is going to change if you don't change; if the things you usually do always worked, you wouldn't need leadership development.

Your Leadership Edge
p 86-93

If the challenges we face are adaptive (and the big ones are) we must make this dimension of Manage Self, *experiment beyond your comfort zone,* a way of life. To make more progress on the things we care about, we need to identify our strengths and go-to moves and then push ourselves to find even more ways to energize more people. We need a greater range of available interventions. In times like those we are currently in, marked by great uncertainty about how to ensure a just, equitable and meaningful future for everyone in our communities, *experiment beyond your comfort zone* must become a way of life for those who seek to lead.

Unlike the more reflective, internal (and related) dimension of Manage Self, *get used to uncertainty and conflict,* this one is active and visible to others as we practice it. In practice, *experiment beyond your comfort zone* means: Find ways to communicate with people you normally don't talk to; listen when you feel compelled to speak; ask more provocative questions; disappoint your own people by speaking on behalf of another faction; surprise them by entertaining a tough interpretation; be empathetic if your typical approach is strategic; think strategically if you tend to put relationships first; *raise the heat* when it would be more comfortable to let people avoid the adaptive challenge at hand.

This dimension lives within the competency of Manage Self because it represents a way of relating to challenging work and a willingness to seize opportunities to intervene in ways that risk revealing our incompetence. Because there are risks involved in doing something different, warn your students not to experiment this way unless they have a strong and compelling purpose for doing so. We stretch ourselves for a purpose. We make ourselves uncomfortable so we can be more effective, in more situations, with more people. We risk looking incompetent so we can make more progress on adaptive challenges.

At the same time, like other dimensions of Manage Self, this is as much about developing capacity to lead in multiple situations as it is about making progress on a particular adaptive challenge. *Experiment beyond your comfort zone* is a behavioral muscle that we can train in low-risk situations as preparation to address our biggest challenges. Encourage students to look for opportunities to build the skill in every meeting that could be more productive, every organizational culture that needs boosting, every human interaction with the potential for greater meaning. Help them stretch outside their comfort zones in supporting others' work as they prepare to be more effective in exercising leadership on what matters most to them.

Activating this dimension starts with self-assessment. Design sessions to guide people in identifying their default behaviors and the strengths they rely on. Help them remember situations where those defaults and strengths didn't work. Have them look to others they admire for possible alternative interventions. Challenge them to imagine a stretch beyond their comfort zone with questions like: What might work instead? How will you manage the fear or discomfort of trying something different? How will you hold yourself accountable for doing something different? Remind them again: If we keep doing things the way we've always done them, we will get the same results.

> **“Sometimes experimenting outside your comfort zone means applying skills that come easily in low-pressure situations to a situation in which you are struggling, maybe where there a lot of emotions involved.”**
>
> **Irene Caballero, KLC Coach**

Objectives

LEVEL 1

1. **Understand** that leadership and progress on adaptive challenges will require you to initiate experiments that are uncomfortable and outside your typical (default) set of behaviors.

2. **Learn** that it only makes sense to experiment beyond your comfort zone if you have a strong and compelling purpose for doing so.

3. **Define** the current limits of your competence, confidence and comfort when attempting to exercise leadership.

4. **Try** something beyond your typical behavior (in the classroom or back in your context) to move a group into the productive zone of work.

LEVEL 2

1. **Identify** and attempt new behaviors and activities that compel you to stretch and build new leadership capacities while contributing to purpose.

2. **Make** purposeful and strategic choices about when to experiment beyond your comfort zone and when to rely on strengths and habitual moves. (It is unwise and exhausting to experiment all the time. If what you are good at will work, do that.)

3. **Notice** systemic pressures compelling people to act within their comfort zones.

4. **Generate** new pressures, relationships, connections to purpose and internal motivation to stretch beyond your comfort zone.

In the real world

A condo association board member who aspires to exercise more leadership feels frustrated by discussion that constantly revolves around technical issues such as dues and trash pickup. She normally says little in meetings but sees the opportunity to experiment beyond her comfort zone. She speaks up to describe ideas she has about how the association could nurture better relationships among residents. She asks who else would like to delve into the topic more deeply at a future meeting and gets a universally positive response.

Q&A

Q: What is the simplest way of explaining the difference between *experiment beyond your comfort zone* and *act experimentally?*

A: *Experiment beyond your comfort zone* is a Manage Self behavior. Much of the work is personal stuff like doing more creative thinking about possibilities, building courage to do something you've never done before, building new skills, evaluating your own risk tolerance, etc. *Act experimentally* is an Intervene Skillfully behavior. It starts with asking questions like: What's my purpose? What would progress look like? What do I need to learn? The two behaviors are related. The answers to the *act experimentally* questions may compel you to experiment outside your comfort zone. As you seek to mobilize others, you may also ask yourself: What would be out of the norm around here and therefore draw attention? How can I show up in a new and unexpected way that could lead to progress?

Resources

Your Leadership Edge, pages 86–93.

When Everyone Leads, *Part Five: Everyone Can Lead.*

Cartoons – Manage Self Package
go.kansasleadershipcenter.org/CT_MS

Worksheets – Manage Self Package
go.kansasleadershipcenter.org/WS_MS

Video – Uncertainty and Conflict
go.kansasleadershipcenter.org/UandC

Colin Gregor writes about getting out of the comfort zone and into the learning zone: go.kansasleadershipcenter.org/zone

Listen to Black Girls Run founder Ashley Hicks as she describes her relationship with running and the valuable rewards behind going beyond one's comfort zone: go.kansasleadershipcenter.org/AshleyHicks

When you regularly *experiment beyond your comfort zone* (Manage Self) you gain a wider range of behaviors to choose from when you *act experimentally* (Intervene Skillfully). Confidence that you can *manage your vulnerabilities and triggers* (Manage Self) makes engaging with this dimension more likely. You must get outside your zone if you want to *work across factions* and *engage new voices* (Energize Others).

Session ideas

1.

Invite individuals to reflect on a time when they stretched beyond their comfort zone and it led to progress: What did you do? How did it feel? What happened? What did you learn? What new capacities did you develop?

2.

Have people coach one another to identify new, potentially productive behaviors to achieve their purpose. Seed the activity with questions like: What would moving beyond your comfort zone look like in this situation? What would the most courageous person you know do? The most empathetic person? The most strategic?

3.

Integrate art and creative play to inspire people to move beyond their comfort zones, or to discover what it feels like to live with the uncertainty of trying something new.

CHAPTER 12

Take Care of Yourself

It is easy to let this dimension of Manage Self, *take care of yourself,* slide off the leadership program agenda when time is tight. Do not do it. Create space in your program to help people reflect, identify, and practice ways to keep from exhausting themselves for a cause, burning out and abandoning adaptive work. Support people to exercise leadership for the long haul by giving them time to assess and adjust the level to which they attend to their own physical, spiritual, intellectual, and emotional needs. This dimension of Manage Self means intentionally fostering the ability to self-regulate, to calm yourself down and cheer yourself up, to live life in ways that allow you to be who you are truly created to be, to lead in the arenas where you want to make a difference most. Don't we want that for everyone we interact with?

Your Leadership Edge
p 94–101

When we do the things that sustain and revitalize us, when we take care of ourselves, we prepare ourselves to exercise leadership more effectively. We encourage people to attend to self-care in four categories: Physical, emotional/social, intellectual, and spiritual. Considering each category, we pose questions like: What habits drain this type of energy? What practices could you replace them with to increase your energy and support your capacity to lead? Those who aspire to exercise more leadership on adaptive challenges must be prepared to return often to the well of their own purpose, and to other sources of strength. They must build time into their lives to reflect on the emotional and spiritual aspects of adaptive work, including the nature of loss, the stress associated with leadership, and the necessity of self-awareness and a clear personal vision for their work in the world.

If you do leadership development at a community or grassroots level, don't underestimate or gloss over basic needs, such as food, housing and security. *Take care of yourself* starts there and may include asking for help when facing layoffs, illness or unemployment.

A few cautionary words for when you teach this dimension. You may have great ideas about self-care, habits that have worked for you for years. Nonetheless, when you teach, avoid sharing those examples with anything other than the lightest touch. This work can backfire if you use your authority to do anything more than draw attention to the need for more intentional self-care and create space for people to see their own ways forward. Design activities that allow individuals to self-assess, reflect on their internal, intimate experience, and remember the habits, places and people that support them in being their very best. Facilitate sharing of self-care ideas among peers and encourage individuals to approach this as they would any other leadership behavior from *Your Leadership Edge*. Be the coach who reminds them not to attempt to change everything all at once. Help people think of changing their self-care habits as they would any other adaptive challenge. There is no quick fix. Instead, experiment: Make a hypothesis (If I go to bed earlier, I will have more energy), design an experiment (I will go to bed at 9 p.m. every night), and see what you learn in the process (9 is too early because it cuts into family time, 10 p.m. is just right).

Help students embrace the idea that, when undertaken for the sake of sustaining your capacity to make progress on tough challenges, self-care is not pampering, it is an exercise of leadership.

> **“When trying to figure how to better take care of yourself consider things that brought you joy as a child or young adult. How might re-engaging with those activities or hobbies help you renew and reinvigorate yourself?”**
>
> Amanda Cebula, Co-author, *Your Leadership Edge*

Objectives

LEVEL 1

1. **Understand** why *take care of yourself* is a leadership behavior.
2. **Reflect** on ways you currently take care of yourself and opportunities to instigate new habits or put a stop to ineffective habits.
3. **Design** and implement one behavior change or activity to take care of yourself. Assess the extent to which this change enhances your willingness or ability to exercise leadership.

LEVEL 2

1. **Understand** the physical, intellectual, spiritual and emotional dimensions of self-care.
2. **Reflect** on the emotional and spiritual aspects of adaptive work.
3. **Clarify** in writing your personal purpose and vision for leadership.
4. **Make** an informed commitment to taking better care of self.
5. **Understand** the power of habit and processes that have proven to work when implementing new rituals for self-care.
6. **Implement** and continually assess a range of behaviors to take care of yourself physically, intellectually, spiritually and emotionally.

Q&A

Q: So, this is about work/life balance?

A: That and much more. This is about making sure you stay healthy and committed to the tough, lengthy, ambiguous work of making progress on adaptive challenges. While a side benefit might be you gain better work/life balance, the purpose is staying engaged in adaptive work.

Q: Some participants worry that *take care of yourself* means adding more to an already full plate. Does it?

A: No. Often self-care starts with deciding what you need to stop doing. You can't make progress on one adaptive challenge if you are spreading yourself thin trying to fix everything that's wrong with the world. Likewise, adding healthy habits doesn't require a grand gesture or big-time commitment. Think of something small that you enjoy doing and start there. A little goes a long way when you are intentional about purpose.

In the real world

During World War II, self-care for British Prime Minister Winston Churchill was two baths, heavy drinking, and a dozen cigars per day. That was what he needed to bring his best to the challenges at hand. Regardless of circumstances, those routines were non-negotiable. They were not luxuries. Our times, too, require leadership for the long haul. Know and indulge your self-care non-negotiables.

Resources

Your Leadership Edge, pages 94–100.

Cartoons – Manage Self Package
go.kansasleadershipcenter.org/CT_MS

Worksheets – Manage Self Package
go.kansasleadershipcenter.org/WS_MS

KLC Guidebook, pages 96–101.

Mindfulness is key to self-care. Start or end your class with a 10-minute body scan. Resources at go.kansasleadershipcenter.org/mindfulness and go.kansasleadershipcenter.org/scan

Boundaries: *When to Say Yes, How to Say No To Take Control of Your Life* by Dr. Henry Cloud and Dr. John Townsend

Burnout: *The Secret to Unlocking the Stress Cycle* by Emily Nagoski, PhD and Amelia Nagoski, DMA.

You'll find great coaching questions and ideas for classroom activities in *The Power of Full Engagement: Managing Energy, Not Time, Is the Key to High Performance and Personal Renewal* by Jim Loehr and Tony Schwartz.

Therapist and trauma specialist Resmaa Menakem walks listeners through a short body practice about race and healing at go.kansasleadershipcenter.org/healing

In one of our short videos, faculty member Jan Davis says, "If you are triggered and taken out of the game, then you can't lead." Taking care of yourself sets you up to *manage your vulnerabilities and triggers* (Manage Self).

Session ideas

1.

Have people fill out the Energy Inventory on pages 98 and 99 in the *KLC Guidebook*. Before they start, let them know this is a data collection tool. Success does not mean checking all the boxes. Celebrate what's working and use the tool to generate ideas about new behaviors. Coach people to get honest with themselves about things that consistently drain energy and develop strategies to give these things less attention. Encourage people to revisit the inventory at intervals. Through life's different seasons, energies shift and self-care evolves.

2.

Have your class read Ed O'Malley's Memo to KLC staff on page 97 of *Your Leadership Edge*. Discuss what resonates. Then, have individuals write their own "Memo to Self" or "Memo to Team" with guidelines for self-care, accountability and how both relate to leadership.

3.

Pair people with a peer coach or accountability partner to support behavior change linked to self-care.

PART THREE

ENERGIZE OTHERS

Remember the leadership principle *it starts with you and must engage others.* The best idea or intervention goes nowhere without others taking up the cause.

No one can tackle a daunting challenge alone. Tell those you seek to develop not to try to carry the load themselves. We have to energize lots of people to take up the work of leadership.

Energizing starts with figuring out where people are coming from: What do they care about, and what do they need? People get energized when they know others care about their situation. To be effective at energizing others, we need to start where others are, to show them we care and listen to what matters most to them.

With complex challenges, one faction can't make progress alone, we have to work to bring them together. Working across factions means purposefully seeking ways to engage new voices rather than relying on the same small group of individuals to develop and implement solutions.

Leadership looks like inspiring a collective purpose big enough to energize all the relevant factions. Energizing others is about acknowledging loss and creating trustworthy processes of engagement.

CHAPTER 13

Engage New Voices

Engage new voices is an essential dimension of the leadership competency Energize Others. When you teach this behavior, create ample space for people to reflect, discuss and discover for themselves why _engage new voices_ is an energizing, rather than diagnostic, dimension of the leadership competencies. Push them to design experiments that allow them to experience the energy that results when new and necessary perspectives get added to the mix of adaptive work.

Your Leadership Edge
p 104–109

With almost every adaptive challenge faced by your students, there is some group they can name—with a bit of prodding from you—that they hadn't considered including before. Perhaps a student thought they didn't need that group's input, collaboration, or interventions. Or maybe they worried that if they start talking to that group it will confuse things, and the adaptive work is complex enough already. Sometimes it has simply never occurred to them before that a certain group of people had a stake in their issue.

Get them to consider the idea that including people who represent atypical points of view will help energize everyone else and move the challenge forward.

"New voices" are those we tend not to engage. Who the new voices are is different for each leadership challenge. The new voices you need may have perspectives or authority to move progress toward purpose in unusual and unforeseen ways.

On the flipside, we use the term "usual voices" to indicate our go-to crew, the people we first think about related to a challenge. They may think like us or have made it clear in the past that we'd better not change certain things unless they are involved from the start. A complex, adaptive challenge will require more new ideas than your go-to crew on its own can provide.

Your Leadership Edge does not equate new (or what we used to call "unusual") voices with marginalized or underserved groups. True, sometimes our conscious or unconscious biases result in failure to include people who are regularly silenced because of their race, ethnicity, income, age, sexuality, gender, or ability. As we diagnose our situation and *identify who needs to do the work,* leadership means pushing past those biases to include people who might bring stories of oppression, exclusion, or just everyday experience with the system we are trying to improve.

However, *engage new voices* points to more than marginalized groups. Often the new voices we need to make progress are those in authority or with the ability to influence budgets and policy. Sometimes they are the people whose opinions we think we know. Other times we fail to realize how a group of people will be affected by a change we seek. Those are different ways of thinking about new voices. Again, who the new voices may be depends on the challenge, as well as the habits and relationships of the person who wants to exercise leadership. Whatever the case, when you skillfully engage new voices, you inject new and often conflicting perspectives, unleashing energy for more interpretations and possibilities for experimentation and progress.

Get your students thinking about how this distinction between usual and new voices tends to play out for them, with the adaptive challenges they care about most. When we bring atypical voices to bear on a problem, we bring new energy to the work. Once we grasp the concept that engaging new voices is an energizing behavior, new possibilities for exercising leadership reveal themselves.

Those who have been using the *Your Leadership Edge* book for awhile will notice a change to this dimension. The first edition of *Your Leadership Edge* uses the phrase "engage unusual voices." Over the years the KLC team has received advice from our closest friends that the word "unusual" was not helpful in elevating the point that new and energizing voices can come from anywhere. Everyone has a role to play in identifying all the relevant voices who need to be engaged to make progress on a leadership challenge.

DEFINITIONS

Usual Voices are your go-to crew, the people you'd typically engage with on a challenge like the one you are facing.

New Voices are those outside your go-to crew, people who have something to contribute (or lose) related to your challenge, but whom you don't typically engage with or attempt to energize or draw energy from.

> **"In some instances, such as social justice or equity and inclusion work, it is important to note that important new voices may be those that deem themselves not impacted by the issue or topic at hand. It is easy to identify 'winners' and 'losers.' It's not so easy to engage and energize those who have no opinion either way. This is how the concept of 'allies' was created."**
>
> Mildred Edwards, PhD, ACC, KLC Coach

Objectives

LEVEL 1

1. **Understand** definitions of usual voices and new voices as used in this dimension.
2. **See** engaging new voices as an energizing move, not a diagnostic move.
3. **Know** that engaging new, atypical voices can help energize other people and get them in the productive zone.
4. **Practice** identifying people who will inject new energy into the work on your challenge.

LEVEL 2

1. **Accept** the value of seeking new and atypical voices to propel the work forward.
2. **Understand** that engaging new voices supports experimenting beyond your comfort zone.
3. **Design** experiments in energizing others by involving atypical voices in a way that is new and perhaps even uncomfortable.
4. **Commit** to do three things in the next three weeks to bring new voices to the table around a challenge.
5. **Experience** the results of engaging new voices (for instance, more meaningful progress and greater sense of purpose).

In the real world

Jay, a manufacturing company president, decided his workforce was unmotivated and lacked a sense of community. He set out to write a new set of company values designed to lift the spirits of the workforce. When his coach suggested he solicit help from his leadership team, Jay declined, saying he knew what they would say and that he didn't want naysayers to have a negative impact. Jay's coach wondered, and urged him to consider, how he might engage the naysayers in a way that was energizing to them and to the overall process.

Q&A

Q: How do I engage new voices in the classroom without alienating the usual voices?

A: Invite the usual voices to pay attention to their own reactions. Ask what they notice physically and emotionally as they quiet themselves enough to make space for a new voice. Another technique is to challenge the usual voices to show up in the room differently, by asking questions or supporting another person's effort to engage.

Q: How do I invite a potential new voice that does not want to be singled out or exposed?

A: Have a side conversation with that person. Share your sense that they have a perspective that would bring needed energy to the group. Ask what they would need in order to feel comfortable sharing it. Maybe, challenge them to experiment by leaning in and sharing their perspective. But leave the choice to them.

Resources

Your Leadership Edge, pages 104–109.

When Everyone Leads, Chapter 23, *Make Leadership Less Risky for Others.*

Cartoons – Energize Others Package
go.kansasleadershipcenter.org/CT_EO

Worksheets – Energize Others Package
go.kansasleadershipcenter.org/WS_EO

KLC Guidebook, *When in doubt, make a faction map.* See page 49.

Check out *The Collaborative Leadership Fieldbook:* *A Guide for Citizens and Civic Leaders* by David Chrislip. It's a hands-on resource for engaging the right people to solve complex community problems.

In a series of eight-minute videos, National Geographic cultural educator Aziz Abu Sarah engages new voices from the Palestine-Israel conflict. Aziz has spent his entire adult life fostering understanding of the complex relations between these two nations and has developed innovative ways to bring together voices with diverging perspectives and overlapping experiences. go.kansasleadershipcenter.org/cz

We gather clues about which new voices to engage as we *identify who needs to do the work* (Diagnose Situation). *Explore tough interpretations* (Diagnose Situation) compels us to understand systemic pressures and patterns that leave some groups behind. *Work across factions* (Energize Others) and *inspire a collective purpose* (Energize Others) help us think about ways to engage. Attempts to *engage new voices* force us to *experiment beyond [our] comfort zone* (Manage Self) and when we've done it once we retain capacity to do it again and again. Likewise, when we fail to *engage new voices*, it can be the inability to *manage your vulnerability and triggers* that gets in the way.

Session ideas

1.

Ask a question and get people talking in small groups: Related to your challenge, what new voices can you engage who would bring energy and perspectives to the group? How might you need to adapt your approach in a way that helps new voices get more comfortable with the idea of speaking up and being heard?

2.

Have each class member identify a person or persons related to their adaptive challenge whom they know very little about. Assign homework to arrange a time to meet just for the purpose of learning more about the person(s) they identified. Remind class members to focus on understanding who the other person is and what they care about. Encourage class members to pay attention to their own energy before, during and after the meeting.

3.

Invite people to engage with the faction map of their adaptive challenge and consider what groups they may not have engaged or considered engaging, whether due to your own triggers or blind spots, or because "that's how we do things around here."

CHAPTER 14

Start Where They Are

"This way!"

This dimension of Energize Others, *start where they are,* acknowledges that there will be people who don't feel the same sense of urgency about your adaptive challenge as you do. There will be groups who have other priorities, and people who are not ready to subject themselves to the loss that could come with change. There will be voices who could have joined you, but instead get raised against you, because you didn't take the time to *start where they are.*

Your Leadership Edge
p 110–115

Start where they are is an energizing behavior that assumes we've done our diagnostic homework. It points to a set of actions that let others know you've done your best to see the world through their eyes. It means experimenting with the words you say, the way you listen, and the processes you create to demonstrate you are willing to let others' priorities influence your own. An experiment with *start where they are* could look like an energizing conversation in which you seek to help people realize that you understand and will do everything you can to mitigate the risks they face by getting involved in your issue.

Start where they are is not a "one and done" leadership behavior. It is a move we need to come back to over and over when doing adaptive work. Especially when uncertainty is high and the situation is changing quickly, it is an act of leadership to continuously display understanding of the attitudes, fears and values of the people who are affected by an issue and need to do the hard work to address it.

Help those you teach and coach draw on their own experience with this dimension of Energize Others. Share stories of times when you failed to take other people's priorities and fears into account and encourage them to remember their own. What happened when they missed that piece of the work? Was it like trying to break through a solid brick wall? With those memories close at hand, it's easy for people to see the value of starting where they are, not where you want them to be.

Encourage people to stay curious about their own ignorance, especially around those whose experience and perspectives differ from their own. Push predominantly white groups, for instance, to build their knowledge of the history and challenges of Black, Indigenous and people of color (BIPOC). In your role as leadership developer, consider how that same history may create unique barriers related to exercising leadership as described in *When Everyone Leads* and *Your Leadership Edge.* Practice starting where they are to energize different factions in your classroom. Be prepared to adjust your examples and the way you talk about leadership to meet the needs and experience of the group you are with.

Likewise, think about the many additional ways in which you'll need to *start where they are* if you hope to energize students to practice a different kind of leadership. Focus carefully, as you design and deliver your sessions, to *start where they are,* not where you wish they were or where the design you intend to use assumes them to be. As with any adaptive challenge, be prepared to shift your approaches as you learn more about their context, including what is on the minds and hearts of the people you seek to mobilize.

Finally, as you teach this dimension, be very clear: While we need to find pathways to work, occasionally, with people whose ideas we resist or reject, *start where they are* is not a call to tolerate injustice or inequity.

> **"When you sense disagreement on an issue, pause to name the factions and from there to build a faction map. Ask those in each faction to stand up and 'put them on mute,' while the rest of the group spends some time diagnosing that faction. What do they value? To whom are they loyal? What are they afraid of losing? You'll know the group is practicing this *start where they are* behavior when the stories they tell about other factions are as compassionate and nuanced as the story they tell about their own faction."**
>
> **Jill Hufnagel, KLC Senior Associate**

Objectives

LEVEL 1

1. **Understand** that other people will not automatically care about an issue or challenge as much as you do.

2. **Learn** and acknowledge the extent to which people come at a situation from different experiences and perspectives.

3. **Practice** demonstrating to a person or faction you wish to energize that you understand what they value and what they stand to lose if they engage with your challenge.

4. **Maintain** disciplined attention over time to track shifts in attitude and energy of those involved in your challenge.

5. **Engage** regularly with individuals and groups who have very different belief systems than you do.

6. **Experience** sharing stories as a strategy for starting where other people are.

LEVEL 2

1. **Do** the personal, internal work to discover aspects of your own history and experience that occasionally make it difficult to *start where they are.*

2. **Understand** how systemic pressures, patterns and roles work to keep individuals and groups from affecting change and progress.

3. **Build** knowledge of challenges faced by marginalized individuals and communities and use it to start where they are.

4. **Experience** the risk that comes with reaching across a divide between you and another person or faction to develop empathy for those you ask to take similar risks.

5. **Collaborate** with factions whose values and loyalties are markedly different from your own for the purpose of making progress on an adaptive challenge.

6. **Experience** the discomfort of working with factions whose ideas you resist or reject, if there is substantial evidence that the work could lead to progress for the common good.

In the real world

A new chamber director knows she needs more involvement from her board to attract and retain businesses in their rural community. But rather than lead with that message she starts by talking with individual board members about what they care about most. She develops a reputation for her habit of asking, "What can I do to support you?" Only weeks into her employment does she begin sharing her thoughts about the role board members can play in making progress on their shared adaptive challenge.

Q&A

Q: So much of this dimension overlaps with aspects of Manage Self, Diagnose Situation and other dimensions of Energize Others like *work across factions*. How do I draw clear lines between these ideas?

A: Don't even try. Let it be messy. These dimensions are just clues to possible ways forward. Offer them to people as inspiration for their own experiments.

Resources

Your Leadership Edge, pages 110–115.

When Everyone Leads, Chapter 20, *Ask Powerful Questions.*

Cartoons – Energize Others Package
go.kansasleadershipcenter.org/CT_EO

Worksheets – Energize Others Package
go.kansasleadershipcenter.org/WS_EO

KLC Guidebook, As with other dimensions of Energize Others, when in doubt, make a faction map. See page 49.

Start where they are requires good listening under pressure. Read *Crucial Conversations: Tools for Talking When the Stakes are High* by Kerry Patterson.

Listen to this interview with Michael Baran, author of *Subtle Acts of Exclusion: How to Understand, Identify, and Stop Microaggression* to glean ideas for intentional acts of inclusion to help when you want to *start where they are*: go.kansasleadershipcenter.org/exclusion

As you teach *start where they are* (Energize Others) emphasize the importance of *know the stories others tell about you* (Manage Self). Those stories will point to barriers or opportunities for moving forward together. Likewise, before attempting to energize, take time to thoroughly *identify who needs to do the work* (Diagnose Situation).

Session ideas

1.

Encourage students to ask curious questions as a way of starting where they are with another faction: What do members of this faction value? To whom are they loyal? What losses do they fear? That high-level curiosity is especially relevant for those who wish to contribute to highly complex and systemic challenges like dismantling racism. It is impossible, for instance, for a white person to start where a Black American is or begin to understand the experience and point of view of a descendant of enslaved people if that white person does not take the time to learn about the history and legacy of racism in the United States.

2.

Use dialogue, film, written cases, podcasts and other media to help people understand the extent to which others come at the same situations from different perspectives. Building on the example of the complex challenge of dismantling racism, watch and discuss films such as "12 Years a Slave," "I Am Not Your Negro," and "Selma" to help students understand the weight of history upon Black Americans.

3.

Engage participants to explore their own roots with this written reflective exercise (designed by KLC Senior Associate, Jill Hufnagel) to personalize the idea of starting where they are. Ask each person to complete this sentence repeatedly (in writing) for three minutes: "I come from..." Debrief by encouraging participants to share their writings with one another initially in pairs and then as a group. Have them look for values and contradictions that enliven their reflections. What are they proud of? Curious about? Surprised by? Ashamed of? What are they discovering as they listen to one another? How do these stories impact how we understand ourselves? How do they influence our ability to start where others are?

CHAPTER 15

Work Across Factions

***Work across factions* is a dimension of the competency Energize Others. It is closely linked to *identify who needs to do the work* (Diagnose Situation), *start where they are* (Energize Others) and, of course, *act experimentally* (Intervene Skillfully). Objectives overlap and the four typically get learned and experienced together. While *work across factions* points to a set of energizing moves, successful faction work requires constant diagnosis. There is what could almost be called a spiritual element to this dimension of Energize Others. We must be open, as we seek to energize other people, to being energized in new directions ourselves. Successful *work across factions* requires a willingness to be changed through our connection with the other, to not simply see but also embrace new perspectives, to question our own assumptions and become willing to prioritize others' values over our own.**

Your Leadership Edge
p 116–123

A faction is a group of people who share common values, are loyal to the same things and share a common orientation to an issue requiring adaptive work. We have found that it is most effective, as you prepare people to *work across factions,* to get them used to describing the other faction as they might describe themselves. Encourage them to use noble terms and words they could use without embarrassment with members of the other faction in the room. We are so accustomed to hearing members of different factions describe one another in derogatory terms on social media and on talk shows that it's worth spending classroom time on activities that allow your students to practice speaking respectfully about the factions they seek to energize.

As you teach *work across factions,* you'll find useful backup in other *Your Leadership Edge* chapters with "purpose" in the title. Help people develop the habit of seeking common ground across factions at the level of shared purpose before seeking agreement on strategies and tactics to support that purpose.

Technical skills from the world of coaching and conflict resolution are useful in working across factions: at KLC we often conduct workshops on powerful questions and active listening as foundations for adaptive work.

As you design sessions around *work across factions,* help students resist the pull to action based only on individual interpretations of what is going on with a faction (personal values of its members, individual biases, etc.). Instead, draw them into discussion of how systemic pressures drive individuals into one faction or another and keep those factions from collaborating effectively. In other words, push people to explore systemic interpretations and then engage in experiments to learn about and eliminate entrenched barriers to progress.

"Ask questions that encourage learners to consider new perspectives. Try not to ask questions that are filled with assumptions like, 'How will you feel if your ideas aren't implemented?' Rather, ask open, sincere questions such as: 'What do you care most about related to this situation? What do you wish other factions and groups understood about you and your beliefs? What do other factions that you need to make progress with care most about? What do you stand to lose if you broaden your sense of purpose to include what they care about?'"

Donna Wright, KLC Teacher

DEFINITIONS

A faction is a group of people who share common values, are loyal to the same things and share a common orientation to the work.

Values are deeply held beliefs related to an adaptive challenge, often based on significant life experience, and revealed through actions and behaviors.

Loyalties describe dedication to a group, place, people or way of doing things that may become barriers to progress on the adaptive challenge at hand. Loyalties often trump values.

Losses are what a faction gives up if progress is made on an adaptive challenge. For example, control, security, prestige, familiarity, etc. People anticipate losses and see risks they are not willing to take.

Objectives

LEVEL 1

1. **Know** the basics of the competency of Diagnose Situation, especially *test multiple interpretations* and *identify who needs to do the work.*

2. **Learn** or review definitions of factions, values, loyalties and losses.

3. **See** the world (and your challenge) differently as factions get elevated around an issue in the classroom or back at home.

4. **Know** that it is usually easier to find common ground among factions about purpose than to agree on strategy or tactics.

5. **Name** other factions in the most noble way possible for the purpose of breaking down barriers and shifting us/them dynamics.

6. **Use** powerful questions to energize and connect with a faction other than your own.

7. **Practice** actively listening to another faction, making sure they experience your empathy with the losses and loyalties that will need to be renegotiated as you work together.

LEVEL 2

1. **Understand** that working across factions comes with risks, including the risk of disappointing your own people.

2. **Understand** that systemic pressures and patterns make working across factions difficult.

3. **Make** and test systemic interpretations about what makes working across factions difficult in your situation.

4. **Experiment** outside your comfort zone to energize people who think differently than you do.

5. **Facilitate** dialogue between two or more factions to generate a sense of shared purpose and direction for action.

6. **Navigate** heated moments of *work across factions* using Manage Self skills.

Q&A

Q: What do you say to people who need to work with stakeholders when there doesn't seem to be any commonality?

A: Help them stay curious and keep looking, if not for commonalities, at least for real understanding of what those stakeholders care about. Have them practice stepping into the work-across-factions space with an open mind, ready and willing to actively listen. Coach them to explore what members of the other faction value and what they stand to lose if change occurs. Perhaps they'll find some commonality of core values. At the very least, push them to fully consider the situation from the other faction's point of view. Shared understanding of competing perspectives can be energizing. With an adaptive challenge, that's progress. Encourage them to be curious about a shared purpose that might require them to loosen their hold on a cherished value.

In the real world

The global pandemic that began in 2020 exposed factions within and around school boards, city councils, and county commissions. Each faction promoted a different set of values, priorities and preferred approaches to progress. Leadership required listening to competing voices and viewpoints as a prelude to energizing them toward a common future.

The best advocacy organizations grow their influence by learning to tell their story in ways that resonate with the policymaker receiving the message. The ask is the same, but the message changes based on the values, loyalties and losses perceived by the receiver.

Resources

Your Leadership Edge, pages 116–122.

Cartoons – Energize Others Package
go.kansasleadershipcenter.org/CT_EO

Worksheets – Energize Others Package
go.kansasleadershipcenter.org/WS_EO

KLC Guidebook, Faction map worksheet on page 49 and elsewhere in the book. See also, *Tips for Working Across Factions* on page 65.

Read about the Collective Impact model for social change, a structured process for working across factions: go.kansasleadershipcenter.org/impact

Explore Amy Edmondson's work on psychological safety when working across factions within a hierarchy where some may be unwilling to speak truth to power: go.kansasleadershipcenter.org/AmyEdmondson

The Othering & Belonging Institute offers a strategy and curriculum for relating to others through deep listening and empathy: go.kansasleadershipcenter.org/belonging

The Action Planning Guide for Promoting Full Community Participation Among People with Disabilities, pages 29–31 on engaging different factions: go.kansasleadershipcenter.org/disabilities

The dimensions of Energize Others are interdependent: Create trustworthy processes and places for people to connect and build relationships across factions. Have a clear purpose in mind that inspires a collective purpose. Starting where they are compels you to get curious about other factions by asking powerful questions.

Session ideas

1.

Challenge your students to fill out a faction map about a real-world challenge, big or small, during the upcoming work week. Demonstrate how to map out an issue on a napkin in a coffee shop, or how to quickly sketch it out on a white board during a team meeting.

2.

Have people identify a community, state, or national challenge, something in the news that most people would have heard about. Ask them to identify factions, values and loyalties that are unique to each faction (that may be impeding progress). Then ask them to look for potential common values. Have them generate ideas about how to move toward shared purpose and strategies all can agree on.

3.

Challenge people to pick one "crossing faction" behavior to practice in the room or between sessions. Set up the expectation that you will check in with them later to find out what they learned from the effort. Follow through by having them pair up with another participant to share what they did and learned.

4.

Have program participants identify factions in the room related to the adaptive challenge of learning and practicing leadership skills together. Are there some who are skeptical about the framework? Some who buy it completely? Others who have dismissed it altogether? Use the faction map in the *KLC Guidebook* to make interpretations about what each faction values. From there, coach students to practice intervening to build bridges between factions.

CHAPTER 16

Create a Trustworthy Process

"So it's basically a matter of each of us doing our job, now, isn't it?"

***Create a trustworthy process,* a dimension of Energize Others, requires both forethought and flexibility. Adaptive work happens over time. It is a process of engaging people who think differently about a challenging situation to find ways to learn and make progress together. The more trustworthy that process, the more energized people will be to work across factions and navigate conflicting loyalties.**

Your Leadership Edge
p 124–129

People in authority often have ready ability to convene people and design processes of engagement. But, in embracing the principle *leadership is an activity, not a position,* we affirm that responsibility for influencing process rests at all levels in organizations and communities. In your classes and coaching engagements, help individuals own their capacity to shape processes that lead to lasting change.

Some processes we design in advance, others evolve. *Create a trustworthy process* is a dimension of Energize Others that requires attention to both planning and evolution. Have your students do good diagnosis and use whatever authority they have to lay things out well from the beginning. And encourage them to stay open and observant to how plans land and how different factions engage. For those with limited authority to convene and organize, make sure they know they can intervene in the moment to make sure important voices get heard and their ideas leveraged. Getting all the right people in a productive zone of work—one where they can address conflicting perspectives and make difficult choices—requires thinking from the beginning about methods of engagement that are trustworthy, transparent, inclusive, and flexible enough to keep things moving. It also means intervening whenever needed to get things back on track.

Create a trustworthy process does not mean you need to make sure everyone trusts everything and everyone before you do anything else. Getting process right isn't all or nothing. Trustworthy processes are those in which people speak up when they feel discounted and where the group addresses conflict quickly as it arises. Trustworthy processes are those in which competing factions have the chance to understand one another, an early step on the pathway to trust.

If you have authority, deploy it to assess your system and practices for evidence of trustworthiness. Look for systemic pressures and patterns that keep people from engaging in adaptive work. Then use your influence to implement procedures and design activities to build trust and open doors. If you have little or no formal authority, build relationships with those who do, and experiment with ways to intervene to make your system more open and inclusive of all the people you will need to meet daunting challenges and thrive.

> **"On July 19th of 2013, I was living in Mexico and received a call from someone I had never met before inviting me to join a civil disobedience that would surface the injustice in the U.S. immigration system. He had read my story about my husband being deported from the U.S. and how me and my son had to leave the U.S. to keep our family together. We were looking for ways to come back home to the U.S. I did not hesitate. The following day, me and my son were at the border meeting with a group of strangers, some were organizers, journalists, attorneys, priests and others who, like me, were going to risk taking part in the civil disobedience. Those were days of intensive training. I was among people I have never met in my life and it would have been exceedingly difficult for me to trust each of those people involved, but I closed my eyes and trusted the process. I ask myself now, what made it trustworthy? I think it started with the transparency of the conversation over the phone. They didn't promise anything, they just explained what the action consisted of, including the risks."**
>
> **Claudia Amaro, KLC Teacher and Civic Facilitator**

Objectives

LEVEL 1

1. **Practice** the foundational skills of asking curious questions and listening actively to people with different perspectives on an issue.

2. **Practice** "going on the balcony" to debrief a process or meeting.

3. **Recognize** characteristics of a trustworthy process.

4. **Notice** characteristics and behaviors that decrease trust in a process.

5. **Understand** that a trustworthy process doesn't mean everyone trusts the process all the time.

6. **Know** a range of ways to intervene to improve the process for adaptive work.

7. **Practice** intervening to improve the process for adaptive work.

LEVEL 2

1. **Know** that undiagnosed or unaddressed process challenges inhibit trust and progress.

2. **Assess** our system for evidence of trustworthiness and to understand the process challenges that may be barriers to progress.

3. **Intervene** in the moment to create a more trustworthy context and process for energizing the factions needed for progress.

4. **Use** or partner with authority to proactively design trustworthy processes.

Q&A

Q: How do I help students or coaching clients differentiate between trusting an individual and trusting the process?

A: They are related, right? It will be difficult to energize people to work across factions if there are deep levels of distrust among them. But it is a mistake to wait to address differences of opinion until everyone trusts everyone else. Help people imagine a process that starts slowly and is based in transparency and listening to understand. Use examples from real life or movies that show the difference between trusting individuals and trusting a process. Remember, too, that blind trust is not a good thing. Even the people we respect most make mistakes. We must be willing to question their interpretations and decisions.

In the real world

When Julie Morath joined Children's Hospital and Clinics in Minneapolis as its new COO, she vowed to dramatically improve patient safety in a system that was already meeting industry standards. As the newcomer, albeit with a high level of authority, she consistently launched conversations with new colleagues from a place of humility and curiosity, reassuring each that "health care by its nature is a complex, error-prone endeavor." Her open-ended questions got doctors, nurses and hospital administrators talking about their aspirations to be as good and as safe for their young patients as they could possibly be. In every encounter, Morath modeled the blame-free, high-accountability culture she envisioned. Meanwhile, she used her authority to put in place processes, like the "Failure Vent Analysis Meeting" giving stakeholders at all levels a trusted space to study accidents immediately after they happened. Through this and other process innovations, she built an every-perspective-counts, we-are-in-this-together, blame-free culture, where working together to avoid accidents and generate ideas became the norm. The hospital succeeded in substantially improving patient safety. To learn more listen to hbr.org/podcast/2019/09/how-a-new-leader-broke-through-a-culture-of-accuse-blame-and-criticize.

Resources

Your Leadership Edge, pages 124–131.

Cartoons – Energize Others Package
go.kansasleadershipcenter.org/CT_EO

Worksheets – Energize Others Package
go.kansasleadershipcenter.org/WS_EO

KLC Guidebook, pages 82–83.

Research by W. Chan Kim and Renee Mauborgne summarized in the *Harvard Business Review*—go.kansasleadershipcenter.org/FairProcess—points to three mutually reinforcing "bedrock elements of fair process" in management contexts. The three principles are engagement (involving individuals in decisions that affect them), explanation (everyone understands the thinking underlying a final decision), and expectation clarity (after decisions are final everyone understands the new rules of the game).

For practical ideas for building trustworthy process check out *The Tactics of Trust* by David Sawyer and David Ehrlichman in the *Stanford Social Innovation Review*: go.kansasleadershipcenter.org/trust

Diagnostic activities designed to *understand the process challenges* and *identify who needs to do the work* support the creation of trustworthy processes, especially if you involve folks who see the problem differently. *Manage your vulnerabilities and triggers* and *get used to uncertainty and conflict* (Manage Self) underline the idea that trustworthy does not mean conflict-free. When we manage ourselves effectively, we allow others to engage more freely. We become better listeners. *Create a trustworthy process* also connects with *take the temperature* (Diagnose Situation) and *raise the heat* (Intervene Skillfully). You must assess the rate of progress and level of engagement before you can attempt to disrupt them.

Session ideas

1.

Start a case-in-point session by stating your assessment that there are hidden issues in the room that get in the way of your collective purpose to learn and practice leadership and not waste anyone's time. Stand your ground. Wait patiently for issues to emerge. Keep people engaged in the discomfort and conflict. Encourage learners to work through barriers to build enough trust, if not in one another, then in the group as a whole. For a description of the case-in-point learning method read chapter 1 in *Teaching Leadership: Case-in-Point, Case Teaching, and Coaching* by Chris Green and Julia Fabris McBride.

2.

Build a session around the tips for creating a trustworthy process on pages 128–129 in *Your Leadership Edge*.

3.

Ask participants to share one thing they want the group to know about them and one thing they would rather the group did not know about them. Making an icebreaker like this one a regular part of your process is an invitation to transparency and, possibly, trustworthiness. Members know they'll have at least one moment to share who they really are in each meeting. Individuals get to choose how much to reveal.

4.

Demonstrate using your position of authority to attempt to create a trustworthy process. Allow the group to make an important decision but use your authority to orchestrate the process by which the decision will be made.

CHAPTER 17

Speak to Loss

"New seating will be perhaps the most visible difference you will see in changing from one-hour days with eight hours of break to eight-hour days with one hour of break."

Speak to loss, a dimension of Energize Others, is about unleashing the power and possibilities that come with acknowledging pain, fear, and loss. No one likes to do it. People in authority are not typically trained to do it. But nonetheless the exercise of leadership on adaptive challenges requires it. Done skillfully, _speak to loss_ is an energizing—though counterintuitive—leadership behavior. If you need to move another faction off the status quo and into a productive zone of work, naming what they stand to lose by getting involved allows them to feel seen and valued. It may even generate hope and fire their engagement with your challenge.

Your Leadership Edge
p 132–139

Help those you teach and coach build courage and skills to acknowledge loss as a way of mobilizing others to do tough, adaptive work.

At a minimum, speaking up about what a group of people fears to lose is like naming any elephant: Truth-telling increases trust and may open the door to a collective sense of purpose.

Learning the distinctions among sympathy, empathy and compassion is good pre-work for practicing *speak to loss*. Sympathy is feeling sorry for another's pain. Speaking to loss from a place of pity will not energize. Empathy, on the other hand, starts with listening deeply to fully understand. Empathy allows us to "feel with" the other person, to stand in their shoes. Compassion pairs empathy with a calm, non-triggered mind. Compassion is an ideal stance from which to attempt to exercise leadership by speaking to loss.

Provide opportunities in your classrooms for people to acknowledge loss with empathy and compassion. Design activities for students to practice listening deeply to the person or group they seek to energize. Coach them to respectfully and compassionately address that loss out loud. Help people practice a range of approaches to this dimension, from creating a process for people to name their own losses, to speaking about another's pain compassionately in public or in a private conversation. As they experiment, debrief the impact of speaking to loss on charged relationships and situations.

Help those you teach see that *speak to loss* is almost always the prelude to another intervention. Encourage them to be thoughtful about what comes next. Perhaps the situation calls for collaboration to help a faction mitigate loss or requires them to slow down, set aside their own immediate plans, and help a segment of the community navigate a difficult passage on the way to something better.

It is worth reminding students that they can't fake *speak to loss.* They can make all the technical listening moves. They can speak the right words to the people who need to hear them, but if the compassion is not authentic, and if students are not willing to reciprocate by sustaining their own losses, people will see it. People will know. Words will not energize other people unless the heart is authentically behind them.

"Speaking to loss is a concrete way to practice how to work across factions. You should work to help a group be more curious about the loss (real or perceived) that is at stake if we make progress on a challenge. Speaking to loss with others is a below-the-neck learning opportunity."

Tim Steffensmeier, PhD, KLC Teacher and Director of Research

Objectives

LEVEL 1

1. **Understand** *speak to loss* as a leadership behavior intended to increase trust and inspire collective purpose by acknowledging what an individual or group stands to lose by engaging in adaptive work.

2. **Understand** that acknowledging and articulating loss can generate disequilibrium and productive engagement.

3. **Practice** empathy and compassion in speaking to loss.

4. **Make** and test interpretations about losses and potential losses with the factions you need to energize.

5. **Create** space to talk about loss, and other things groups normally struggle to talk about.

6. **Practice** a range of ways to *speak to loss.*

LEVEL 2

1. **Acknowledge** the risks associated with naming and inviting people into conversation about loss.

2. **Realize** that, for members of communities who have historically been discriminated against, talking about loss may trigger re-experiencing the loss, with accompanying trauma, sense of hopelessness or frustration.

3. **Practice** asking permission before discussing loss in certain situations or groups.

4. **Practice** identifying and seizing opportunities to speak to others' losses.

5. **Use** understanding of the others' loss to inform your next intervention.

6. **Practice** managing self in discussions about your own losses related to a challenge.

7. **Experience** the relationship and difference between the technical moves associated with acknowledging loss and authentic attempts to build connection and propel progress.

In the real world

A middle manager discovers unproductive tension between the small marketing team she is part of and the larger sales team. She begins thinking about how to intervene to build bridges between the two factions and decides to experiment with *speak to loss*. In a series of casual one-on-ones, she asks questions about what might be lost if the two teams set strategy and celebrated successes jointly. Her marketing teammates reveal how proud they are of their team's reputation as small, scrappy and speedy. The team lead even admits, "We might eventually have better results if we worked more closely with sales but the effort won't be worth it if my job isn't fun anymore. I've put so much time into building these relationships within marketing. I don't want to ruin it." The middle manager listens and empathetically reflects back what she hears, adding, "Yes, I can see how that would be a loss not only for you but for other members of the team." All the while she ignores her instinct to urge him to consider the benefits of closer collaboration with sales. Three days later, however, she notices the marketing team lead, sitting at lunch with his counterpart from sales, smiling broadly and leaning in.

Q&A

Q: How can I get people to recognize the importance of acknowledging loss in a culture that is usually focused on winning? Why should my students *speak to loss* when they suspect it will just give people further ammunition to resist change?

A: Failing to *speak to loss* doesn't make it go away. Once spoken the loss may not feel as big. It may lose some of its power to hold people back from engaging in adaptive work. If your students are happy with the current culture that is all about winning, you may not have a case. But if they want something different, something more supportive of the common good, encourage them to try speaking to loss.

Resources

Your Leadership Edge, pages 132–139.

KLC Guidebook, Faction map worksheets on page 36, 49 and elsewhere throughout the book provide space to consider and prepare to *speak to loss.*

Cartoons – Energize Others Package
go.kansasleadershipcenter.org/CT_EO

Worksheets – Energize Others Package
go.kansasleadershipcenter.org/WS_EO

It takes emotional intelligence (EI) to see, acknowledge and help others work through loss. Daniel Goleman did the research, coined the term and makes useful links between EI and leadership.

Watch this brief video introducing the concept of "bridging" as a strategy for relating to others through deep listening, empathy, and recognition of suffering. go.kansasleadershipcenter.org/belonging

Understand the distinction between empathy and sympathy. According to Brené Brown, empathy fuels connections, while sympathy drives disconnection. go.kansasleadershipcenter.org/EvS

Helping people learn about *speak to loss* (Intervene Skillfully) is important if you want to *give the work back* (Intervene Skillfully). If you are in an authority position and start changing your approach to providing protection, direction and order, people in your organization might experience some loss. Likewise, speaking to loss is part and parcel of *work across factions* (Energize Others). The leadership competencies and dimensions are, of course, all connected. It will be difficult to bring any effort to a satisfactory conclusion if we fail to *speak to loss.*

Session ideas

1.

Drill this dimension using mini cases. Present a situation they could imagine encountering in their work and ask people to come up with three approaches designed to energize others by acknowledging loss.

2.

Make *speak to loss* personal by asking students to reflect on a time they underwent substantial growth or change as a person. What was lost? What was gained? How might that experience relate to this dimension of Energize Others?

CHAPTER 18

Inspire a Collective Purpose

***Inspire a collective purpose* is a dimension of Energize Others. If *inspire a collective purpose* was a road sign it would be to remind us that, when doing adaptive work, we need multiple and creative ways to encourage people to join together to achieve the (seemingly) impossible.**

Your Leadership Edge
p 140–145

When we hear the phrase *inspire a collective purpose* it may, at first, conjure the image of a charismatic person—a John Kennedy or a Martin Luther King, Jr.—whose soaring rhetoric stirs a crowd to embrace a vision and follow their lead. That is just one approach to *inspire a collective purpose.* Sometimes soaring rhetoric is exactly what the moment calls for. But if the work is adaptive even the most talented and visionary among us will need more than one way to energize.

When we choose to exercise leadership, we are not signing up to implement a quick fix and walk away a hero. Adaptive work requires collaboration across factions and always takes time. A collective purpose is one that evolves as people with different viewpoints become engaged in the work. Finding collective purpose is about hard decisions that prioritize one value over another. Finding collective purpose requires people to take risks, deal with uncertainty and tolerate loss. So sometimes *inspire a collective purpose* looks less like soaring rhetoric and more like curiosity and humbly letting go of something you hold dear.

People get energized when someone makes them care more about making progress on an issue than they do about their own comfort. So, yes, *inspire a collective purpose* includes big gestures and bold challenges of people who cannot know if they are up to the task. (Think Kennedy's 1962 speech at Rice University: "We choose to go to the moon in this decade and do the other things, not because they are easy, but because they are hard, because that goal will serve to organize and measure the best of our energies and skills, because that challenge is one that we are willing to accept, one we are unwilling to postpone, and one which we intend to win.")

Other times the moves associated with this dimension are less bombastic, like negotiations with someone whose talents match the needs of the project. Still other times *inspire a collective purpose* is about listening as another faction finds a way to embrace the work and watching as pieces of your original vision fade and disappear as a result.

There is a personal piece to this dimension too and it overlaps with *take care of yourself* from the competency Manage Self. As you teach and coach, help people find ways to regularly reconnect to the personal purpose that drives their adaptive work and may become hidden under cynicism, scars and exhaustion. We can't energize others or *inspire a collective purpose* if we lose track of our own reasons for doing difficult work.

> **"When teaching this dimension, do not forget the power of hope. To inspire people is to give them hope. If your purpose does not compel them to come out of their norms, your good idea will fail to get off the ground. I find effective vision casting (or hope-giving) critical, especially when leading volunteers. Hope is their compensation."**
>
> **Dioane Gates, KLC Teacher, and Civic Facilitator**

DEFINITIONS

Vision means a vivid mental image of a desired future. A vision can change as diverse factions join and inform the adaptive work.

Purpose is what you believe in, the why that informs your desired future, the cause that fuels your vision.

Strategy is the general approach and combination of activities and resources designed to accomplish your larger purpose.

Tactics are the actions, programs or services you choose as part of your strategy.

Objectives

LEVEL 1

1. **Understand** that a collective purpose is one that energizes people from multiple factions to work together.

2. **Know** that inspiring a collective purpose starts with knowing who needs to be engaged to make progress, identifying what is important to each faction, and where their values overlap.

3. **Recognize** and begin to practice a range of methods for inspiring a collective purpose.

4. **Practice** asking questions and listening actively to detect common and divergent purposes.

LEVEL 2

1. **Know** the definitions of and distinctions between vision, purpose, strategy and tactics.

2. **Understand** that finding common purpose may require letting go of favorite strategies and tactics, or some treasured vision of the future.

3. **Practice** inspiring people to care more and do more to make progress on a shared purpose.

4. **Experience** the energy and impact of divergent factions uniting for a collective purpose.

5. **Practice** helping a group notice when collective purpose has shifted or changed.

In the real world

The only two school buildings in a rural Kansas community had fallen into disrepair. As the school board contemplated the way forward, two increasingly polarized factions came to the fore. There was the "build a new and fabulous consolidated school building" faction and the "repair the existing buildings and spend as little money as possible" faction. After some initial missteps, the school board appointed a task force of trusted community members with equal representation from the two warring factions. The chair of the task force was a member of the "repair" faction but had credibility with both sides. Meetings were open, transparent and efficient. People listened to one another and asked questions. Teachers and administrators reported feeling that their opinions were well-considered. The quality of the process inspired a collective purpose among task force members and the larger community. Each side gave up a lot of what they wanted. The community gained two well-equipped and secure schools for 21st century students.

Q&A

Q: What do I tell people who get frustrated with the circular and time-consuming nature of defining collective purpose?

A: Put up with the frustration of today to birth the better reality of tomorrow. Purpose must be revisited and restated often. By the time a few people are tired of talking about it, others are just starting to own it. And if you are the one who originally proposed the way forward and now team members are stating it differently or in words that are even better than yours, purpose has begun to take flight. One person's vision has inspired a collective purpose.

Resources

Your Leadership Edge, pages 140–145.

When Everyone Leads, *Part One: Identify the Gap.*

Teaching Leadership: Case-in-Point, Case Studies and Coaching, Coaching questions, page 185.

Cartoons – Energize Others Package
go.kansasleadershipcenter.org/CT_EO

Worksheets – Energize Others Package
go.kansasleadershipcenter.org/WS_EO

KLC Guidebook, page 81.

Anyone teaching this idea needs to be familiar with Simon Sinek's TED Talk, Start With Why: go.kansasleadershipcenter.org/why

Check out chapter 21, Inspire People, in *The Practice of Adaptive Leadership* by Ronald Heifetz, Alexander Grashow and Marty Linsky.

Take a look at the brief case study of an African American church that successfully mobilized its member families and the broader community around the collective purpose of improving high school graduation rates among young people of color: go.kansasleadershipcenter.org/GradRates

The word "purpose" is the most repeated word in the KLC principles and competencies. *Inspire a collective purpose* (Energize Others) and *hold to purpose* (Intervene Skillfully) go hand in hand. *Make purposeful choices* (Intervene Skillfully) reminds us that difficult decisions are only worth making with a clear purpose in mind.

Session ideas

1.

Case-in-point is a great method for getting a group to practice inspiring a collective purpose. As one faction pushes ahead and unites around a purpose, they can easily leave another group behind, checked out and disengaged. Debrief to highlight interventions that moved the group forward toward a shared understanding of purpose.

2.

Teach storytelling skills to group members and apply them to the work of inspiring collective purpose.

3.

Look to African American literature and history for lessons in how to inspire collective purpose. Contrast the poem "Harlem" by Langston Hughes with Dr. Martin Luther King, Jr.'s "I Have a Dream" speech. Look at interventions by today's activists too. Invite students to explore ways in which people they admire, past and present, have inspired a collective purpose.

PART FOUR

INTERVENE SKILLFULLY

If we keep doing what we have always been doing, nothing is going to change.

If we want to make progress, we must intervene. Intervene Skillfully is the fourth of four leadership competencies. Individuals and organizations intervene into systems to attempt to make progress on things they care about. Help students be intentional about when, why and how they intervene into a system. Teach them to resist doing whatever feels most natural and instead *make purposeful choices* about interventions to meet the moment.

People who excel at intervening skillfully calculate how best to capture the attention of their desired audience. They understand and appreciate the role of conflict in making progress on daunting issues. They are willing to *raise the heat.* Skillful interveners avoid the temptation to take on all the work alone. As you teach, provide opportunities for people to practice giving the work back by empowering all the necessary factions to get involved and to get things done.

Intervene Skillfully is the riskiest of the competencies. That's why a key dimension of this competency is *act experimentally.* When we intervene skillfully, whatever we attempt, we do it in the spirit of curiosity. Model the belief that with adaptive challenges there is no such thing as failure, only learning and inspiration for the next experiment.

CHAPTER 19

Make Purposeful Choices

"We eat brains because brains are for eating. What more is there to think about?"

This dimension of Intervene Skillfully, *make purposeful choices,* is about action with intention. It is yet another reminder that leadership without a clear sense of purpose is an impossibility. Leadership requires timely decisions and purposeful action.

Your Leadership Edge
p 148–155

Leadership is about making choices, often between action and inaction. Too often well-meaning people who say they want to exercise leadership fail to make the necessary, purpose-driven choices. They hedge. They look to someone else. They avoid the work. A clear decision followed by action comes with risk. No matter how skillful, a decision draws attention. It provokes even as it seeks to energize. It invites others to assess our diagnosis and deride our attempts at leadership. Yet, if we want to make progress on tough, adaptive challenges, we must decide. Without decision, there is no skillful intervention, no provocative action, no experiment to generate learning. There is no progress without hard choices. We can't make change if we don't decide.

This dimension points to a range of behaviors. What constitutes a good purposeful choice depends on the situation, the quality of information available, and the practitioner's level of authority, scope of expertise, willingness to risk, and access to useful relationships. In every case, however, a conscious choice grounded in purpose, logic, good diagnosis, understanding of competing values, and clarity about who needs to be engaged stands the best chance of success.

There are elements of self-management and diagnosis tightly bound to this dimension of Intervene Skillfully. Making unpopular choices or intervening for a purpose, when standing back is simpler, takes the will to *experiment beyond your comfort zone.* Likewise, *make purposeful choices* is not a move we make once and then we're done. As with every other leadership intervention, even the most purposeful choice is an experiment to see if we can learn or make progress on what we care about. A skillful intervention always includes a pause to collect data, review the situation and then make your next move.

If you are a longtime student and teacher of the ideas in *Your Leadership Edge,* you will notice that this dimension has been revised. Previously titled *make conscious choices,* it is now *make purposeful choices.* Analysis by KLC staff and teaching team during our 2020 curriculum renewal process revealed: (1) Alumni wanted more explicit direction about how to Intervene Skillfully; and (2) our team had avoided teaching make conscious choices because we had failed to define the behavior precisely enough. Without the necessary precision this dimension became some fuzzy cross between *choose among competing values* (a Manage Self move) and *act experimentally* (an Intervene Skillfully move described in detail later in this book).

However, a return to the origins of this idea—to what Kansans told KLC way back in 2007 about what it takes to make progress on tough adaptive challenges—exposed more depth. Kansans said that to mobilize people to make more progress on things they care about they need to be more willing to make hard choices based on clear purpose. Now more than ever, students need your assurance that—when the situation demands it—making a tough, unpopular decision is a leadership behavior.

> **"As you encourage participants to plan ways to intervene skillfully and work together to make hard choices, resist the temptation to allow the group to settle for the first point of consensus. Encourage the group to dig deeper and name new perspectives, pros and cons of the initial decision. What implications come from exploring unusual and challenging perspectives? What interpretations might the group make about itself? What more purposeful choice might the group make given these new insights?"**
>
> **Lalo Muñoz, KLC Teacher and Civic Facilitator**

Objectives

LEVEL 1

1. **Understand** that leadership requires making choices grounded in a sense of purpose and followed by action that reflects the choice.

2. **Understand** that a purposeful choice stands the best chance of leading to skillful intervention.

3. **See** how this behavior looks different depending on the situation and the practitioner's level of authority in the system.

4. **Feel** on the hook, when dealing with an adaptive challenge, to regularly make purposeful decisions with limited information.

5. **Prepare** to answer the question (related to your adaptive challenge), "What will you do?"

LEVEL 2

1. **Experience** making and following through on a decision that impacts multiple people.

2. **Experience** managing self through a difficult choice.

3. **Practice** making choices under pressure and with too little information.

4. **Practice** making choices related to adaptive challenges when you have authority and when you don't.

Q&A

Q: Who really needs to learn this?

A: People with decision-making power. While much of leadership involves staying in diagnosis longer—engaging multiple factions, hearing multiple perspectives, and building shared purpose—at some point, if things are to move forward, a person with authority needs to make choices about things like budget, pace of the work, human resources, etc. When the work is adaptive there are no "right" choices. There are risks with deciding on one experiment over another.

Q: Who else really needs to learn this?

A: People with no formal decision-making power. Those folks get to choose how to manage themselves and experiment outside their comfort zones. They get to decide how much risk they are willing to tolerate. They get to choose when to exercise leadership. Failing to decide to attempt to intervene skillfully is work avoidance. It is the antithesis of leadership.

In the real world

West Virginia drew kudos in early 2021 for its quick and efficient COVID-19 vaccine rollout. Instead of opting in immediately to the federal plan for reaching people in nursing homes, public health officials in the state made purposeful choices to go their own way. They saw that most seniors lived hours from the big national chain pharmacies central to the federal plan. West Virginia intervened skillfully, activating a network of locally owned pharmacies to swiftly get vaccinations in the arms of people who needed them most.

A congregation sees an ever-increasing number of homeless families in the neighborhood surrounding their church. Determined to take a holistic approach to helping adults care for their families, the congregation makes the purposeful choice to halt its soup kitchen and redirect resources to a new partnership with another downtown denomination. A few months later the two congregations open a homeless shelter and job training program.

Resources

Your Leadership Edge, pages 148–154.

When Everyone Leads, Chapter 9, *Quick Fixes Don't Work.*

Cartoons – Intervene Skillfully Package
go.kansasleadershipcenter.org/CT_IS

Worksheets – Intervene Skillfully Package
go.kansasleadershipcenter.org/WS_IS

Read *HBR's 10 Must Reads on Making Smart Decisions* with the featured article "Before You Make That Big Decision..." by Daniel Kahneman, Dan Lovallo, and Olivier Sibony. The article illuminates the ways in which cognitive biases can override purpose and strategy.

For helping groups make purposeful choices together see *Facilitator's Guide to Participatory Decision Making* by Sam Kaner.

***It's risky* is a leadership principle.** Any decision you make on a tough adaptive issue is bound to be difficult. However, everything will stay as is unless you decide to intervene. Clearly, *make purposeful choices* (Intervene Skillfully) is related to *choose among competing values* (Manage Self). Often, choosing to move forward means choosing between two things you hold dear (equity and inclusion for all versus your own safety and security, for instance). Name those values, if only to yourself. Be truthful. Acknowledge what you are giving up when you choose one over the other.

Remember the principle: *Leadership is about our toughest challenges.* Be clear with yourself about what makes leadership worth the effort, and subsequent decisions come more easily.

Session ideas

1.

Have people use the Act Experimentally worksheet (page 42 in the *KLC Guidebook*) to brainstorm ways to proceed with their adaptive challenges. Work in pairs to assess purposefulness and risk. Hold one another accountable to embark on at least one experiment within the week.

2.

In your classroom, draw a name from a hat and charge that person with making the final choice about what the group does next. For 10 minutes, brainstorm a list of possible activities to move the group forward. Do not screen for what seems plausible or likely. Simply identify as many action steps as possible. Next, push the group to continue to add possible choices for another full five minutes with emphasis on creativity. Finish with one more two-minute push for more ideas with emphasis on stretching the group's creativity. Then, have small groups discuss and each make a recommendation about a way forward. Remind them that the goal is to be purposeful, maximize learning, and make progress with a moderate amount of risk. Use your authority to inject some heat. Remind them: "Resources are limited. There is only time for one experiment." Once each group has made its recommendation, give the decider 90 seconds to decide. Once they've announced the decision, wait five minutes and hit pause. Debrief the experience.

CHAPTER 20

Raise the Heat

***Raise the heat* points to a set of leadership behaviors that force people to deal with conflict and invent new ways forward. Skillful application of heat compels people to pay attention to an adaptive challenge long enough to navigate their differences, reflect on their own priorities, and do what it takes to create lasting change.**

Your Leadership Edge
p 156–161

• • • • •

Raise the heat, a dimension of Intervene Skillfully, means doing something to generate enough discomfort that other people feel compelled to act. *Raise the heat* means disrupting the status quo for a purpose. Dissatisfaction with the present and conflicting views of an ideal future are part of adaptive work. We *raise the heat* to get people to engage in ways they'd rather avoid.

Ron Heifetz and Marty Linsky introduced our team to a metaphor and accompanying visual called the "productive zone of work" that we continue to use in teaching *raise the heat* (see our adaptation on page 191). Heat, in this metaphor, is what happens in groups when we focus attention on issues that are value-laden, with conflicting perspectives. The productive zone of work is the place where there is enough heat (aka discomfort or disequilibrium) that the right people are engaged around a shared purpose. If those people stay in the productive zone long enough, or return there often enough, they can make progress on a common adaptive challenge. Most people want to avoid conflict, to look the other way. We *raise the heat* to get them to pay attention, to make it less comfortable to avoid than to look at the problem. We *raise the heat* when we try to get folks to reconsider their attitudes and practices and re-evaluate their priorities. We *raise the heat* to get people into the productive zone so they will do adaptive work.

Teach people that they can never know for sure whether an intervention will *raise the heat,* or how high it will go, unless they try something. Remember the leadership principle: *It's risky.* Keeping people in the productive zone requires sustained curiosity, frequent provocation, and repeated experimentation. Skillful intervention to raise and maintain the heat is based on careful diagnosis and a willingness to manage oneself along the way.

At Level 2 when teaching this dimension, we explore unique opportunities available to people in positions of authority to intervene to move people into the productive zone. Those in authority can give permission for people to abandon task lists and set aside technical work to focus on a daunting adaptive challenge. They can provoke, leverage, highlight an important purpose and create processes and environments that enable people to tolerate the discomfort that comes with change.

Sometimes, though, the heat gets too high for the people you seek to engage. The problem is too scary, or emotions are too raw. People are angry or panicking. Then, instead of raising the heat, leadership means taking steps to calm things down. Wise use of authority is finding ways to lower the temperature so people can breathe and think and get ready to listen to other points of view. When heat is too high and things are no longer productive, partner with authority or use your own to rebuild trust, acknowledge feelings, and re-create a stronger holding environment for change.

When helping people learn and practice this dimension, you may choose to emphasize *raise the heat* or, for more conflict-averse groups, you can enter through the doorway of "managing the heat." Either way, remind people this is not about raising heat for heat's sake, discomfort for discomfort's sake. As you design your sessions, realize there is a lot for students to digest around this dimension. Don't plan to work through all the Level 1 or Level 2 objectives in a single session. Learning and practicing leadership is adaptive work. *Raise the heat* slowly, over time, if you want the learning to stick.

DEFINITIONS

Heat, in the context of leadership and mobilizing people to do adaptive work, is a synonym for discomfort. The optimal level of heat gets the right people engaged and making progress toward a common purpose.

Optimal Heat = Shared Purpose + Engagement + Progress

The **productive zone** is metaphor for circumstances in which there is enough heat that the right people are engaged with enough of a sense of shared purpose to keep them engaged and a general sense that they are learning and making progress on that shared purpose.

Progress means forward movement on an adaptive challenge and is the desired outcome of an act of leadership. Progress is not always immediately evident. Progress may include learning or insight, including from an intervention that did not go as planned.

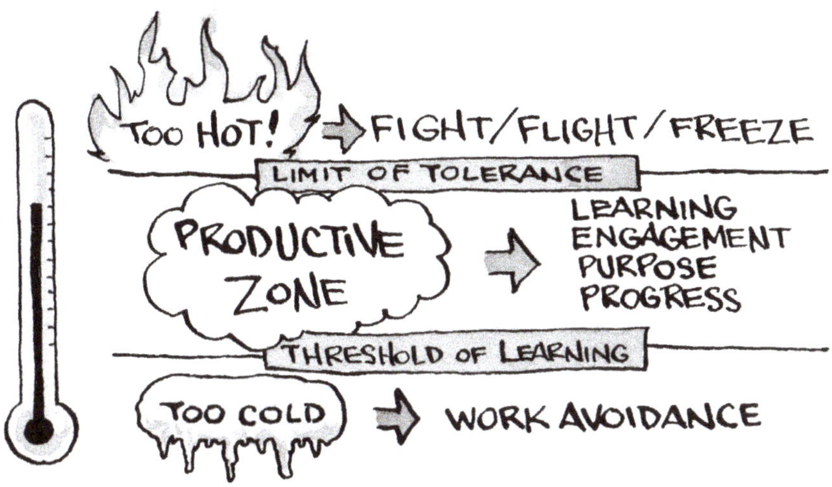

Objectives

LEVEL 1

1. **Understand** that if sustainable progress is to be made there will be discomfort.

2. **Know** the definition of heat and why we need to generate heat to create and sustain change.

3. **Understand** the productive zone metaphor and see the productive zone as a place of curiosity, provocation, and experimentation.

4. **See** the link between *raise the heat* (Intervene Skillfully) and *get used to uncertainty and conflict* (Manage Self).

5. **Identify** interventions that can be counted on to raise or lower the heat.

6. **Understand** that raising the heat is only appropriate when there is a clear purpose for any resulting discomfort or loss.

7. **Contrast** possible consequences and risks of raising the heat versus opting not to raise the heat related to an adaptive challenge.

8. **Experience** what it's like to be in a place of disequilibrium that is both productive and uncomfortable.

LEVEL 2

1. **Explore** the role of authority in moving people to the productive zone.

2. **Explore** what it takes to create environments in which people have greater tolerance for the discomfort that comes with adaptive work.

3. **Accept** imperfection and failure as necessary risks of purposefully attempting to *raise the heat.*

4. **Assess** current risks of keeping heat low (related to an adaptive challenge).

5. **Assess** our own level of willingness to take risks (accept casualties, lose status, etc.) related to a specific challenge.

6. **Experiment** to keep people in the productive zone related to an adaptive challenge.

7. **Intervene** to raise awareness when pressures in a system keep heat low and maintain status quo.

“Prior to convening a group, spend some time thinking through the heat the group is coming in with. This will be key to calibrating the heat and assessing how much heat the group can tolerate. Questions to consider before you meet the group include: When were they last together and what happened then? How well do group members know one another? What recent losses/challenges/traumas has the group faced? What is going on in their context/industry? What is top-of-mind for them? With this background in mind, then consider: What are the authority relationships in the room? What's the goal of the session? How long will you be together? Are they avoiding important adaptive work? Who is doing the hard work of leadership? The answer to these questions will drive both the design of the session and the interventions that will help the group make progress.”

Jill Hufnagel, KLC Senior Associate

In the real world

Employees at a small company are known for strong team spirit and eagerness to innovate. However, the COO is frustrated by a general inability to see projects through to completion. In an effort to build a culture that values getting things done as much as it values teamwork and entrepreneurship, she directs each employee to identify a single quarterly objective. Those objectives are shared publicly, and results get measured and reported at the end of each quarter. More focus on results equals more heat around accountability. After some initial anxiety and discombobulation, the COO starts to see progress. Projects are getting done faster and, in many cases, better.

Late civil rights leader and congressman John Lewis understood the need to raise the heat. He knew from experience that discomfort and tension are necessary to move forward. Read about his optimistic vision for social change through good, necessary trouble: time.com/5087349/why-getting-into-trouble-is-necessary-to-make-change.

Q&A

Q: Why do some people insist on equating heat with conflict?

A: Because they hate conflict so much they'll avoid getting anywhere near it. It is true that when you attempt to *raise the heat* you typically elevate conflicting perspectives, conflicting values. But with adaptive work, that is progress. No way around it. You must go through it. KLC research shows that when a system saturates itself with leadership development, and when people understand the purpose of raising the heat and dealing with conflict, they begin to see adaptive challenges as opportunities, rather than barriers to their work. Help your students and coaching clients celebrate bringing conflict out of the closet and into the light of day.

Resources

Your Leadership Edge, pages 156–161.

When Everyone Leads, *Part Four: Use the Heat.*

KLC Guidebook, *Managing the Heat,* page 38; *Nature of Leadership and Authority,* page 62; *Raise the Heat,* page 87.

Teaching Leadership: Case-in-Point, Case Studies and Coaching
Chapter 1 – *Case-in-Point Teaching,* pages 35–67; coaching questions, page 178; Session 8 – *Intervene Skillfully: Raise the Heat,* 228–232.

Cartoons – Intervene Skillfully Package
https://go.kansasleadershipcenter.org/CT_IS

Worksheets – Intervene Skillfully Package
go.kansasleadershipcenter.org/WS_IS

For a host of real-world examples of how businesses build the capacity of individuals and teams to tolerate heat, read *Adaptive Capacity: How Organizations Can Thrive in a Changing World* by Juan Carlos Eichholz with a foreword by Marty Linsky.

Get Peter Senge's take on "holding creative tension" in his book *The Fifth Discipline: The Art and Practice of the Learning Organization.*

Raising the heat to compel a system to do adaptive work demands Manage Self skills like *get used to uncertainty and conflict, choose among competing values,* and especially *experiment beyond your comfort zone.* What difficult decision or unpopular action might be necessary? What might be uncomfortable? What actions might generate necessary conflict?

Session ideas

1.

Debrief a class session (or team meeting) using the productive zone visual (see page 191). Have the group look backward and chart where it was during key moments. Ask individuals to answer questions like: Where were you on the chart at this point during the session? At this other point? Then chart it all for the group to see. Did the group work together to make progress toward a shared purpose? What took them below the productive zone? How did they recover when things got too hot? What would they do differently next time?

2.

During a virtual class, assign partners to chat privately. Encourage these partners to diagnose where the heat is, bounce ideas off of one another about what the group needs, and support one another to intervene to turn up the heat without causing harm to self or others.

3.

If you are working virtually, pause and ask people to rename themselves according to how engaged they are in that moment. Encourage the group to work together to get as many people into the zone as they can. Help the group identify ways they individually and collectively turn the heat down. Do they rely on Lee's humor? Expect Araceli to take care of the group when feathers might be ruffled? Does the group avoid the hot topics until the end of a session?

4.

Encourage individuals to identify a purpose worth experimenting for and an action that has been on their edge that they will experiment with to raise the heat and generate progress in the group.

CHAPTER 21

Speak from the Heart to the Heart

Speak from the heart to the heart means be vulnerable about your own feelings and experience for the sake of moving an issue. It means inviting others to be open and honest about feelings as well. When the work is adaptive, emotions, deeply held beliefs and difficult past experiences are part of the process. Welcome heartfelt communication. Bring your heart to the challenge. Be open with the people you seek to engage.

Your Leadership Edge
p 162-167

Important update to Intervene Skillfully: *Speak from the heart* is now *speak from the heart to the heart.* We have edited to prioritize impact. Your intervention is not skillful unless your words resonate with others. Sharing feelings and experience in ways that touch another's heart and cause them to do something different requires practice. Be ready to reveal your emotions when the moment requires vulnerability. When possible, rehearse your story ahead of time for maximum impact. But practice cannot mean dishonest. People smell deceit a mile away. And never let communication be a one-way street. Even as you open your heart, first let other people know you see, hear and understand their needs and emotions.

Develop the capacity to deeply listen in those you teach and coach. Likewise, help those you seek to develop understand they may not be able to fully empathize with individuals and factions who have experienced trauma and marginalization. Help them choose when to *speak from the heart to the heart* and when to find other ways to intervene. When emotions are high, or bubbling beneath the surface, it's easy to get triggered into speaking first and listening later. Urge students to practice self-awareness, to notice when they get anxious or defensive, to be wary of needing to play the expert, to believe others when they say they are not ready to be vulnerable. Always, this dimension starts with listening. Sometimes, listening is all there is.

On another note, there is a thin line between speaking from and to the heart to move a challenge forward and connecting heart to heart for the sake of building relationships. They employ many of the same skills. The difference between friendship and leadership is purpose. If someone you care about has lost their job, for instance, and doubts their ability to find another, you can remind them of tough times they've faced before, of people like you who are always in their corner and about how you've seen them grow and thrive in the face of past adversity. You may have to remind them again and again before they find it in their heart to believe in themselves. That's friendship in action.

Speak from the heart to the heart becomes a leadership behavior when you do it within the context of a larger vision that involves working across factions and staying strong together as you endeavor to make progress on a collective adaptive challenge. Take, for instance, a community facing hard times, high unemployment and sagging confidence that things will get better. Imagine you want to exercise leadership to help that community embrace an asset-based approach to its future development. In that case, you may need to speak from your heart to groups of all sizes, and have repeated conversations with key individuals where you reach for and resonate with something in their hearts that says, "Yes, we have what it takes to turn this place around."

Objectives

LEVEL 1

1. **Understand** why *speak from the heart to the heart* is a leadership behavior and dimension of Intervene Skillfully.
2. **Identify** examples of effectively speaking from the heart to another person's heart.
3. **Learn** and practice technical skills for speaking from the heart to the heart.
4. **Observe** and make interpretations about the impact of your experiments with speaking to the heart.
5. **Explore** what makes this hard.

LEVEL 2

1. **Acknowledge** the feelings and values of another faction when they run counter to your own.
2. **Understand** that you may not be able to fully empathize with some individuals and communities and that some other intervention may be needed.
3. **Open** your heart; be vulnerable yourself; notice when you get defensive.
4. **Encourage** your team to practice speaking to the heart.
5. **Pair** this behavior with efforts to Energize Others.

"We can almost make a math problem of it: Loss > Purpose = Resistance. It's human nature to pay more attention to what we fear we'll lose than what we stand to gain. Vital to speaking to someone else's heart is your ability to see resistance not as some form of stubbornness, but instead as a longing to avoid the deeper pain of change and loss. Help groups explore the losses they will have to weather to make progress. Have the group surface and acknowledge those losses. Then ask: What purpose would be compelling enough to accept those losses? This is the kind of conversation that helps create opportunities for speaking from and to the heart."

Jill Hufnagel, KLC Senior Associate

In the real world

On December 29, 2020, *The Wichita Eagle* newspaper ran an article headlined: "Getting COVID vaccine is matter of life and death, Black doctors tell Wichitans." Quotes from doctors in a virtual town hall demonstrated a range of examples of *speak from the heart to the heart*. For instance, Dr. Rita Stanley referenced the seven principles of the African cultural holiday of Kwanzaa, especially unity and responsibility. "When I say I want to live," said Stanley, "I'm really saying I want to live for me and the people around me. I want to live for the children and the older people. I want to do what is right for me by getting the vaccine." Dr. Dennis Onentia Oyieng'o used a story. He said, "Today I was just seeing a patient, and he was telling me: 'I'm tired, I'm tired of breathing. I can't do this anymore.' ... When you look in his face, you can see a lot of despair. Initially when he came in, he was very optimistic. But right now as the disease is catching up with him and he's getting weaker and more short of breath, you can sense in him that he's sensing that maybe death is imminent. You can look in his eyes and see his fear, that he's afraid of what's coming."

Q&A

Q: What do I say to people who question the change in wording of this dimension? Isn't *speak from the heart* enough?

A: One way to think about it is that *speak from the heart* was too technical. It was more about delivery than impact. (Tell the right story and tell it well.) *Speak from the heart to the heart* makes the work adaptive. It requires the person seeking to exercise leadership to embrace an experimental mindset about whether and how their words touch the people they wish to mobilize. Do the words reach the heart? Does something change in the listeners? Does someone else feel compelled to join in the adaptive work?

Resources

Your Leadership Edge, pages 162–167.

Cartoons – Intervene Skillfully Package
go.kansasleadershipcenter.org/CT_IS

Worksheets – Intervene Skillfully Package
go.kansasleadershipcenter.org/WS_IS

Brené Brown's work on vulnerability is essential for anyone who believes real leaders don't show emotion or weakness. See her famous TED Talk or read *Dare to Lead: Brave Work. Tough Conversations. Whole Hearts.*

Storytelling skills workshops allow groups to experience the power of speaking from one heart to another. We recommend Annette Simmons' book, *The Story Factor: Inspiration, Influence, and Persuasion through the Art of Storytelling.*

Master coach Marcia Reynolds brings *speak from the heart to the heart* into the coaching relationship in her book *Coach the Person, Not the Problem: A Guide to Using Reflective Inquiry.* Or check out the interview with Marcia on the *Be Awesome at Your Job* podcast: go.kansasleadershipcenter.org/ri

Read *Fierce Conversations:* *Achieving Success at Work and in Life One Conversation at a Time* by Susan Scott.

Check out leadership coach Sabina Nawaz's blog post about framing your message at go.kansasleadershipcenter.org/one

Listen to (or read) this conversation between Krista Tippett and Lucas Johnson from the *On Being* podcast as they engage with the question: "Who are we going to be to each other?"

Session ideas

1.

Heifetz, Linsky and Grashow in *The Practice of Adaptive Leadership* talk about tapping into the song beneath the words when attempting to engage another person in adaptive work. Design a session in which people practice getting to this subtext by repeating a partner's words and phrases. Coach them to choose to repeat back metaphors, words that connote feeling, or any language that strikes them as especially powerful. If the partner echoes back, they know they are on to something. Partner with them to unpack their words and learn more about what matters most and what words may be most impactful when they attempt to *speak from the heart to the heart.*

2.

When working with someone who is facing a difficult situation, notice how much of what the person says is coming from above the neck—the rational, logical, cognitive, cerebral stuff—versus what is coming from below the neck, in the heart and gut. Share back some of what you've heard and then invite the person to pause for a moment to share what's going on below the neck. Ask: What would it take to give more airtime to your heart? What would it take to listen more for what's going on in another's heart? What makes that tough?

CHAPTER 22

Give the Work Back

"Okay, now what?"

***Give the work back,* a dimension of Intervene Skillfully, is essential practice for people in positions of authority and anyone who lives by the maxim "if you want it done right do it yourself." With adaptive challenges, no one can do it alone. As the principle says, it starts with you and must engage others. Put another way, it starts with you but to make real progress you must *give the work back* to those best suited to do the work.**

Your Leadership Edge
p 168–175

Giving the work back means admitting that you don't have all the answers. It means engaging other people from the start to describe an adaptive challenge from all the necessary perspectives. It means convening people so they can explore interpretations and design experiments together. It means listening, rather than delegating, as people discover and describe their piece of the work. It means evaluating the work together and consistently sharing the activity of leadership. If the work is adaptive, no one can do it on their own. Progress requires other people feeling compelled, usually by growing discomfort with the status quo, to do their part to move a challenge forward.

People will resist invitations to engage in adaptive work, so *give the work back* is not a single intervention. People happily cede important decisions to experts or look to people in authority so that they don't have to risk stepping out themselves.

Give the work back does not mean delegating. Delegating is when a person with supervisory or managerial authority directs another person to do something technical. With delegation the supervisor can describe a clear path and be confident about the outcome. Delegating is often necessary yet delegating is technical work.

Give the work back, on the other hand, is adaptive work. *Give the work back* is a leadership activity. *Give the work* back encourages another person, or another faction, to design their own leadership experiments. *Give the work* back requires a level of humility—

especially from people in authority—to admit, as Reggie Robinson said so eloquently in the video referenced on page 212, "I don't know," and "I don't have all the answers."

Give the work back is asking others to engage in the difficult activity of leadership. So, warn the people you seek to develop that they can't just toss the work to someone then turn away and hope for the best. Coaching skills come in handy in helping others step up, assess the situation, design experiments, and navigate potential losses that come when they take on adaptive work.

> **"Pressure is high on people in authority to have all the answers, solve all the problems and keep systems running efficiently and effectively. Burn-out is real. It's almost surprising to me to see how much my clients hang on to. They are so afraid of giving adaptive work to the people who must do the work, or so trained to take on everything themselves. They even risk their health and well-being."**
>
> Joyce McEwen Crane, PhD, PCC, KLC Teacher and Coach

Objectives

LEVEL 1

1. **Understand** that no one can solve an adaptive challenge on their own.
2. **Know** that *give the work* back means involving all necessary factions to make progress on an adaptive challenge, and that all necessary factions must be mobilized to exercise leadership.
3. **Know** the three phases of giving the work back (diagnosis, implementation, evaluation) and some ideas for accomplishing it in each phase.
4. **Practice** making distinctions between work that is yours to do and that which belongs to others.
5. **Experience** the uncertainty that comes with letting go of attachment to particular outcomes when you *give the work back.*

LEVEL 2

1. **Understand** the systemic pressures that tend to push work back to authority or experts.

2. **Explore** your role and behavior, especially if you are in a position of authority, in situations where you've failed to *give the work back.*

3. **Help** others navigate the change and loss that comes when they take on adaptive work.

4. **Practice** giving the work back from a position of authority for the purpose of building a culture in which people at all levels embrace the leadership principles and practice the competencies described in *Your Leadership Edge.*

In the real world

Progress on population level health outcomes requires people in authority to give the work back. Yes, you need experts for technical work like developing vaccines, drafting policy, and implementing best practices. But individuals and families must find their own ways to live with the policies and practice those behaviors for a community to get healthier. If you had authority for some aspect of public health, how would you begin to give the work back?

Q&A

Q: Why do we say that *give the work back* is different than delegating?

A: Delegating assumes that (1) you have the authority to tell someone else what to do and (2) using it is the right move to make progress on the adaptive challenge. The pressure is great on people in authority to "solve" the adaptive challenge and delegate the details of execution to others. If you hold the authority position, others expect you to lead the way, alleviate risk, take initiative, solve problems, seize opportunities and move the system forward. Giving the work back means you avoid that trap. You recognize you can't do adaptive work alone. Giving the work back is not abdicating responsibility. Giving the work back means setting the system up for sustainable change by engaging and energizing other people to do work only they can accomplish. You'll be most successful if you engage others right from the beginning. Give them the work of diagnosing the situation and describing the problem from their perspectives.

Resources

Your Leadership Edge, pages 168–174.

Teaching Leadership: Case-in-Point, Case Studies and Coaching – Chapter 1 – *Case-in-Point Teaching,* pages 35–67; coaching questions, page 178.

Cartoons – Intervene Skillfully Package
go.kansasleadershipcenter.org/CT_IS

Worksheets – Intervene Skillfully Package
go.kansasleadershipcenter.org/WS_IS

Matt Andrews, public policy lecturer at the Harvard Kennedy School of Government, made this short video about "giving the work back to the people who should do it." go.kansasleadershipcenter.org/gtwb

In *Solving Tough Problems,* Adam Kahane writes that it's the people who have the problem who need to be the ones to fix it. He shares a framework for building the capacity of those involved to acknowledge their role in the challenge.

Foster community participation to build accountability and give the work back to people who are prepared to take it. Find tools and methods at go.kansasleadershipcenter.org/reflection

In his talk, *Energizing Others at the Intersection of Leadership and Authority,* KLC founding board member Reggie Robinson makes the case that *give the work back* is the hardest and most critical dimension for those in authority positions: go.kansasleadershipcenter.org/Reggie

Before you *give the work back,* you'll need to *identify who needs to do the work* (Diagnose Situation). A scattershot approach won't do the trick. Instead, *make purposeful choices* (Intervene Skillfully). Have good reasons for letting go of the work and resist temptation to take it back.

Session ideas

1.

Have people practice the steps and behaviors for the three phases of giving work back outlined in the Give the Work Back chapter (pages 171–173) in *Your Leadership Edge*.

2.

Make time for students to list work they now see should be given to others. Help them develop plans for energizing those people. Anticipate what level of direction and protection they may need in order to commit the necessary time or take the risk to exercise leadership. Encourage students to identify possible obstacles such as the urge to micromanage or treat the handoff as a technical move of delegating tasks.

CHAPTER 23

Act Experimentally

It all comes down to this. We make progress on adaptive challenges when we *act experimentally.* Experiments can be big or small. Whether we succeed or fail doesn't matter as much as what we learn and how we use it to inform the next experiment. We can experiment to manage ourselves, to diagnose the situation, to energize other people. We can experiment in or outside our comfort zone, whatever it takes to make progress on the challenges facing our communities, companies and organizations. We experiment to make the world a better place for ourselves and those we love.

Your Leadership Edge
p 176–181

An experiment is an action, behavior or internal shift made purposefully to learn or make progress on an adaptive challenge. We design experiments to collect data about our challenge and the system surrounding it. We design experiments to engage others and catalyze change. Adaptive work requires multiple, successive experiments.

A single experiment is rarely, if ever, sufficient to solve an adaptive challenge, though a series of experiments may result in lasting change.

An experimental mindset is perhaps the primary characteristic of cultures, systems and individuals who regularly and successfully exercise leadership and make progress on adaptive challenges. Experimental mindset drives the Observation-Interpretation-Intervention cycle introduced in the section on Diagnose Situation. Experiments fit within the cycle in at least two places. First, we experiment to test *multiple interpretations* and identify who needs to do the work. Then, in the intervention part of the cycle, we design higher-risk or more resource-intensive experiments to engage others, *work across factions* and produce the future we desire.

An experimental mindset does not get hung up on failure; and it only seeks opportunity to learn. Experimental mindset involves constant attention to small, low-risk experiments to test interpretations about the best way forward, and subsequent bigger experiments greater opportunity for sustained progress and success.

As your students start thinking about even the smallest, least risky experiments, remind them of the leadership principle *leadership is about our toughest challenges.* A high-quality experiment has solving a tough challenge or achieving a bold aspiration as its end goal. Encourage your students to consider what they hope to learn from the experiment and how they will use the data to inform what they do next to make progress on their challenge.

After you've taken action and an experiment is complete, go back to the cycle at Observation, ready for more diagnosis and the next attempt to catalyze movement and change. The four leadership competencies and the dimensions within each provide myriad ideas for experiments. Encourage students and coaching clients to return to the *Your Leadership Edge* book when they feel stuck and need inspiration for their next experiment.

In your classroom or coaching relationships, the question, "What experiments have you run in the last 4-6 weeks?" will generate accountability for exercising leadership among those you seek to develop. Don't let people get away with not experimenting. If they bother to show up for leadership development, if they aspire to make more of a difference or want to move up in their company, hold them accountable for experimenting.

DEFINITIONS

An **experiment** is an action, behavior or internal shift made purposefully to learn or make progress on an adaptive challenge.

Experimental mindset describes a person or system that consistently implements experiments to test interpretations to learn and discover the best way forward with adaptive challenges. Experimental mindset includes an attitude of no failure, only opportunities to learn.

> **"Whenever possible, have learners review their experiments with peers. People can create some risky and overwhelming experiments. An objective perspective can help increase the chances the experiment will be put into action and then lead to learning and progress. Asking for one or two volunteers to share their experiments with the full group and carefully going through each step while interacting with the learner can help others refine their experiments. Coaching is a great way to build accountability related to the experiment. Ask questions about what was observed, new interpretations, and next interventions. But remember, this is not a technical step-by-step process. As you coach, elevate potentially competing values, explore risk, cultivate curiosity, and promote a sense of 'being experimental' rather than simply cranking out and doing experiments."**
>
> Kevin Bomhoff, ACC, KLC Senior Associate

Objectives

LEVEL 1

1. Know the definition of an experiment in this context.

2. Understand that experiments can be big or small, public or private, and involve varying levels of risk.

3. Know that adaptive work necessitates a series of experiments.

4. Know where experimentation fits in the Observe-Interpret-Intervene cycle.

5. Design experiments including:

    - Purpose for the experiment.
    - What you'll do.
    - What you expect to learn and/or the progress you expect to see.
    - How you will use the result as data to inform your next experiment.

6. Evaluate the level of risk associated with an experiment, including the level of intended heat.

7. Feel energized around trying something with a new experimental mindset.

8. Establish individual accountability for experimentation during and after the leadership program.

LEVEL 2

1. **Recognize** the pressure to maintain the status quo in systems and how it works to derail or diminish experimentation.

2. **Act** experimentally to keep a group in the productive zone.

3. **Design** experiments with a clear hypothesis and specific actions.

4. **Experience** learning from a first experiment, making interpretations and implementing subsequent experiments, following the O-I-I cycle continuously toward satisfactory progress on your adaptive challenge.

5. **Encourage** others in your system to think and act more experimentally.

6. **Establish** team and organizational accountability for experimentation.

Q&A

Q: How do I handle concerns from participants about not having enough time in their day or week to do experiments?

A: Differentiate between doing experiments and being experimental. We are not suggesting adding new work. *Your Leadership Edge* is about addressing existing challenges with a different mindset. Encourage your participants to make themselves curious learners engaged in finding out what works and doesn't. That mindset leads to time better spent. Also, lower the difficulty level. Help learners develop small, simple experiments they can conduct in a matter of days or a couple of weeks.

Q: What do I say to students who are worried about looking incompetent or people in authority whose colleagues expect them to have all the answers?

A: Remind them not to experiment if the problem is technical and they have the authority or expertise to fix it. But if the challenge has adaptive components, competence is not enough to make lasting change. We must act experimentally.

In the real world

People in hierarchical organizations or that rely heavily on authority may need to spend time imagining what acting experimentally looks like in their context. It does not have to feel like a subversive act. Instead, they can discuss their purpose for experimenting and the steps involved with their supervisor and team. Even when their experiment pushes against authority or the organization's culture, conversation helps alleviate the risks.

Some industries use an experimental model to address tough technical challenges. They adapt by experimenting to learn when existing procedures fail. However, they don't think to apply those same skills to address organizational challenges. Help people transfer existing skills to a different category of challenges.

Resources

Your Leadership Edge, pages 176–181.

When Everyone Leads, Chapter 22, *Everyone Can Act Experimentally.*

KLC Guidebook, page 81.

KLC Guidebook, *Act Experimentally,* page 42, 102–103 and 109; *YLE Leadership Dashboard,* page 46.

Teaching Leadership: Case-in-Point, Case Studies and Coaching, Chapter 1 – *Case-in-Point Teaching,* pages 35–67; *coaching questions,* page 180; Session 9 – *Intervene Skillfully: Act Experimentally,* 233–235.

Cartoons – Intervene Skillfully Package
go.kansasleadershipcenter.org/CT_IS

Worksheets – Intervene Skillfully Package
go.kansasleadershipcenter.org/WS_IS

Acting experimentally and the Observe-Interpret-Intervene cycle have close connections to continuous improvement models. Businesses and health care providers are familiar with the Plan-Do-Check-Act (PDCA), Kanban, Lean methodology or Deming cycle. Don't hesitate to highlight these similarities. It legitimizes the approach.

All other ideas and behaviors from *Your Leadership Edge* connect with this one. When designing experiments, make sure learners go back to the KLC framework for inspiration and to the *Your Leadership Edge* book for tips and suggestions.

Session ideas

1.

As a leadership developer you need ready examples of challenges you've faced and experiments you've designed and carried out. Make sure these are not "one-and-done" examples (I experimented, it worked, and we were done). That way you can demonstrate that adaptive work requires a cyclical, Observe-Interpret-Intervene approach.

2.

Use the Observe-Interpret-Intervene visual (page 44 of this book) to underscore the need for multiple experiments.

3.

Watch the newspapers for stories of community activists or business-people who try one approach and then, based on what they learn, change course and are more effective in subsequent efforts. See if you can name their purpose, the hypothesis they were operating under, actions they took, and what they learned that led to the new course of action. Use this activity to elevate the experimental nature of leadership.

CHAPTER 24

Hold to Purpose

Hold to purpose means maintaining focus—when the work is hardest—on where you are going and why it matters. There is an element of _hold to purpose,_ too, that is about keeping other people focused, helping them remember why all the hard stuff is worthwhile. Leadership on a daunting adaptive challenge will require active experimentation and repeated heat-raising to keep people from getting distracted. It takes sustained focus on purpose, by all the necessary stakeholders, to create lasting change.

Your Leadership Edge
p 182–187

Leadership doesn't happen without purpose. You can't emphasize it enough. The word 'purpose' shows up in *Your Leadership Edge* yet again in this dimension of Intervene Skillfully, hold to purpose.

It is important to acknowledge the creative tension between this idea and *inspire a collective purpose,* a dimension of Energize Others. *Hold to purpose* is about actively and repeatedly demonstrating and calling others to the focus and conviction necessary to move an adaptive challenge forward. *Inspire a collective purpose,* on the other hand, is about constant curiosity and experiments to make the purpose as big and inclusive as it can get. Don't try to resolve the tension between these two dimensions for yourself or your students. Just know there will be times when one set of moves is required and other times you'll need the other. As you teach this dimension, remind people that they don't get to choose between *inspire a collective purpose* and *hold to purpose.* With adaptive work, it's both. Press them to identify a purpose big and broad enough to inspire people from other factions—people with some different values, loyalties, and potential losses—to join in the adaptive work of achieving it.

Too often people conflate purpose with strategy or tactics, or they hold so tightly to a vision of success that they cut off the air of possibility for everyone else who needs to be involved. Purpose is the reason we take up a challenge. It is the gap we seek to illuminate; the disparity we must eliminate; the driver of our vision for a better future. Strategy is the general approach to accomplishing a larger purpose. Tactics are the details for getting the strategy done. When the work is adaptive, we will be most successful if we *hold to purpose* while staying super-flexible about strategy and tactics. *Hold to purpose* and invite others to co-create the strategies.

Vision, too, is best held lightly. With adaptive work, we start at A eager to get to our desired Z. But as new people get engaged and as we learn and experiment, the vision changes so that instead of going from A to Z, we end up somewhere else entirely and wouldn't wish it any other way. Help your students see that they can hold to purpose, even as other factions bring their experience to bear on the challenge and even as a vision of success transforms to fit the needs of that growing constituency.

Purpose comes in a variety of different time frames. Deep daunting challenges—like childhood poverty or racial justice—call people to years, even lifetimes of holding to purpose. Founders spend decades growing a small business for the purpose of sustaining family and serving community for generations to come. On the other hand, improving the efficiency of meetings in your organization may take some technical adjustments followed by two or three months of intervening to make sure you and others are implementing them. Whatever the situation, a purpose worth holding is one that is broad enough to engage the factions you need to make progress and personal enough to fuel and sustain you through the ups and downs of leading.

DEFINITIONS

Vision means a vivid mental image of a desired future. A vision can change as diverse factions join and inform the adaptive work.

Purpose is what you believe in, the why that informs your desired future, the cause that fuels your vision.

Strategy is the general approach and combination of activities and resources designed to accomplish your larger purpose.

Tactics are the actions, programs or services you choose as part of your strategy.

"In KLC's *Your Leadership Edge* program we can count on energy rising when we ask people to pair and share their purpose for wanting to make progress on their adaptive challenge. It is difficult to get them to stop talking because they are so deeply engaged in talking about purpose. Purpose is energy to fuel the activity of leadership."

Mary Banwart, KLC Teacher and Researcher

Objectives

LEVEL 1

1. **Understand** that an effective purpose is broad enough to engage the various factions needed to make progress on an adaptive challenge.

2. **Understand** that holding to purpose means maintaining focus, as you attempt to exercise leadership, on what you value and seek to accomplish.

3. **Know** that purpose comes in a range of sizes (from purpose of this meeting to mission of our organization).

4. **Engage** others in conversation about purpose.

5. **Experience** the range of opportunities to exercise leadership that come with a clear purpose.

LEVEL 2

1. **Know** the definitions of and distinctions between vision, purpose, strategy and tactics.

2. **Realize** that when the work is adaptive you'll more successfully engage others if you hold to purpose while staying flexible about strategy and tactics.

3. **Practice** articulating purpose so others can understand and embrace it.

4. **Practice** energizing others to hold to purpose.

5. **Feel** confident in being able to identify, hold, and return to purpose when doing adaptive work.

Q&A

Q: How do I help people define a purpose they can hold to long enough to make progress on the adaptive challenges within it?

A: Purpose must be directional and aspirational. Often, at first, their purpose is either too abstract or too narrow. Rarely, unless they have given it a great deal of thought, does it hit at the level where it has both direction and aspiration. When it is too abstract it is easy to walk away from; when it is too narrow it's less likely to inspire others. While this dimension is about holding to purpose, taking time to get clear about purpose is essential. In your classroom, reinforce the need to step back, reflect and effectively articulate purpose. When they can articulate their purpose and deeply understand it themselves, they have something worth holding on to.

In the real world

A KLC team member was coaching the director in a unit of more than 30 client-facing employees. Everyone on the team was deeply committed to client service. However, some were also deeply loyal to outdated processes the director was determined to change. The processes created inefficiencies and ultimately fostered a toxic work culture. This director is an excellent problem-solver and aspirational planner, but much less comfortable with conflict and disappointing people. She knew there would be unhappy team members, comfortable with the status quo. Before a pivotal meeting, the KLC coach helped the director articulate her purpose and the values imbedded in it. They talked about how those values connected with priorities of each faction with the unit. With a clear purpose in mind, the director reported little nervousness going into a meeting where she had to deliver news others would not like. In that and subsequent conversations, even when a few team members chose to leave the unit, the director kept reminding herself the change was in service of their clients, their team and the mission of the organization. She held to the purpose she'd articulated.

Resources

Your Leadership Edge, pages 182–187.

When Everyone Leads, Chapter 13, *Start With Your Challenge*.

KLC Guidebook, page 81.

KLC Guidebook, page 107. See also page 102, where the exercise asks participants to identify purpose when *acting experimentally* and page 81 for thinking about inspiring a collective purpose.

Teaching Leadership: Case-in-Point, Case Studies and Coaching, Chapter 1 – *Case-in-Point Teaching,* pages 35–67; *coaching questions,* page 179.

Cartoons – Intervene Skillfully Package
go.kansasleadershipcenter.org/CT_IS

Worksheets – Intervene Skillfully Package
go.kansasleadershipcenter.org/WS_IS

Check out *The Practice of Adaptive Leadership* by Ron Heifetz, Alexander Grashow and Marty Linsky, pages 236–238, for classroom activities about holding to purpose.

Explore the work of Marshal Ganz on using stories to help people connect with purpose go.kansasleadershipcenter.org/lcn

Inspire a collective purpose (a dimension of Energize Others) and *hold to purpose* (Intervene Skillfully) go hand in hand. A purpose worth holding to has enough depth to inspire across factions. In other words, your purpose needs to serve more than your own ambition.

Session ideas

Challenge participants to articulate and deepen their understanding of why they want to make progress on their adaptive challenge. Pair them up and have the listener ask, "Why?" at least three times. Then switch roles. Debrief with questions like: As the person repeatedly being asked to state your purpose, what did you notice that was different in each round? What did you learn about your purpose? As the listener, what did you notice? What does this have to teach us about holding to purpose?

Onward

The purpose of this teacher companion is to energize your efforts to equip people to make progress on complex, adaptive challenges so our organizations, companies and communities can thrive. Our fondest hope is that your leadership development interventions release people from the story that "someone else will do it."

We envision you using this teacher companion (in concert with your teaching and coaching skills, stories, examples, and experience) to build cultures where *everyone* leads.

We imagine you coming back to this book every time you embark on a new leadership development relationship. Open it for inspiration or for a quick refresher. Open it when you have only a short time with a group. It will help focus your choices and use that time wisely. Use it as a conversation starter with leadership development colleagues. Use it as a tool to support your good work in the world.

Let the *Your Leadership Edge Teacher Companion* be a foundation for helping people see and solve tough challenges. Let it inspire and sustain you in your important, world-changing work.

We offer it not as a rule book or set of directions, rather as a leadership intervention to energize you to take more risks and have more impact. Get curious about what your participants need most and get creative about how you deliver it. This book is our way of giving the work of designing sessions back to you. Make it a touch point of clarity and inspiration as you design sessions that fit your context.

When a group of people come together to learn and practice leadership, they are engaging in adaptive work. You are right there in it with them. You may be at the front of the room or in the coach's seat, but your work is adaptive too. As the person in authority, you need to embrace the principles from *When Everyone Leads: How the Toughest Challenges Get Seen and Solved* and apply the leadership behaviors in *Your Leadership Edge.* You have the responsibility to diagnose the process challenges and look for ways to make sure that every faction feels engaged and implicated in the work of the group.

You'll need to *make purposeful choices*. You'll need to *choose among competing values* and experiment in the midst of the action to create a process that people trust enough to make themselves vulnerable, to open themselves to the possibility of doing something different.

Do it your way. Push yourself and push your participants to embrace the leadership principles and practice the competencies. But keep in mind that there is a limit to your authority at the front of the room, just as there are limits to the expertise we can offer in this book.

Developing leadership capacity in others is adaptive work.

Enjoy! Experiment! And let us know what you learn.

Acknowledgments

This was a group project. Thanks goes first to all of the KLC staff and contractors who participated in the in-depth review and renewal of our curriculum undertaken in the winter of 2019 and spring of 2020. They are Mary Banwart, Kevin Bomhoff, Seth Bate, Thane Chastain, Brittany Engle, Chris Green, Lynette Lacy, Tim Link, Ashley Longstaff, Idalia Loya, Joyce McEwen Crane, Kaye Monk-Morgan, Julian Montes, Lalo Muñoz, Ed O'Malley, Adrion Roberson, Shaun Rojas, Tim Steffensmeier, Racquel Thiesen, Katy Weidner, DJ Whetter, and Donna Wright.

I appreciate everyone who provided detailed feedback on the manuscript in semi-final form. Your clear-eyed wisdom is embedded here: Kevin Bomhoff, Irene Caballero, Thane Chastain, Mildred Edwards, Brittany Engle, Andy Huckaba, Jill Hufnagel, Tim Link, Teresa Schwab, and Astrid Villamil. Mo Sook Park merits special gratitude and recognition. Her depth of knowledge about the leadership ideas in *Your Leadership Edge,* about Adaptive Leadership, systems thinking, racial justice and the challenges of exercising leadership in a complex world is exceeded only by the quality of her feedback and timeliness of her provocative questions. It was impossible to avoid folding her insights into this book and Mo generously allowed me to do so.

Claudia Amaro, Seth Bate, Amanda Cebula, Phyllis Collins, Andy Huckaba, Howard Keim, Patrick Kelly, Tina Khan, Joyce McEwen Crane, Jonathan McRoy, Lalo Muñoz, Tim Steffensmeier, and Donna Wright reviewed specific chapters, offering edits, ideas and perspectives.

Thanks to David Chrislip for insights related to the curriculum renewal process, especially the push to include the voices of participants in KLC programs. Thank you to the alumni who responded to our surveys about what was working, and not working, with the leadership principles and competencies in *Your Leadership Edge.* Thanks especially to directors and facilitators of local community leadership programs for your perspectives. You influenced this project at the beginning and near the end. I hope you find the product useful for your work. Nothing is as powerful as local leadership development applied to real cases where people live.

Brandon W. Kliewer, PhD, and Kerry L. Priest, PhD, colleagues from Kansas State University's Staley School of Leadership Studies, contributed a pivotal white paper offering new lenses through which we viewed the KLC curriculum.

Chris Green, managing editor of The Journal, contributed substantive reflections on the civic context as have been revealed to him through the pages of KLC's quarterly magazine. The KLC board of directors and its chair, David Lindstrom, weighed in thoughtfully about the how the context for civic leadership has changed since KLC was founded in 2007.

Founding KLC CEO Ed O'Malley suggested that this material needed to become a book and chief of staff Jamie Moeder helped free up time and budget to bring it to fruition. Thanks to members of the KLC staff who tend to operations, finance, and communication: Damon Young, Tyrena Judie, Shannon Pope, and Sam Smith, your hard work makes so much else look easy. Joy Panos Stauber, thank you for your collaboration on this fresh and inspiring book design. Your enthusiasm for the project got us over the finish line.

Special thanks to Marty Linsky for the mid-course conversation about purposeful intervention, and for many challenging conversations over the years. You temper wisdom with kindness every time.

Ron Heifetz defined the term "adaptive challenge" and I love his definition of leadership as "mobilizing people to do difficult work and thrive." Thank you for that word "thrive," for the love in it, and all it says about why we do this work of developing leadership capacity in others.

I want to acknowledge each person who has ever purchased and dog-eared a copy of *Teaching Leadership: Case-in-Point, Case Teaching and Coaching,* which I co-authored with Chris Green. You give us hope that there is a special and mighty audience for this book. May it fire your creativity and inspire new ways to reach those you seek to energize through your work.

Doing most of this writing from home during 2020 and early 2021, I was fortunate to have inspiration, support and company from Bill McBride, Lake McBride, one dog, 11 cats, nine chickens, 30-some supersized goldfish, a round robin of (socially distant) bonfires with neighbors in Matfield Green, Kansas, and tallgrass prairie as far as the eye can see.

This is dedicated to the memories of Reggie Robinson and Thomas Stanley.

About the Author

Julia Fabris McBride is chief leadership development officer at the Kansas Leadership Center, where more than 15,000 people around the world have attended programs since 2007. A certified coach, former actor, and co-author of *When Everyone Leads* and *Teaching Leadership,* Julia splits her time between Wichita and Matfield Green, Kansas.

About the Authors of *Your Leadership Edge*

Ed O'Malley is president and CEO of the Kansas Health Foundation. He founded the Kansas Leadership Center in 2007, serving as president and CEO for 15 years. A former Kansas state legislator and gubernatorial aide, Ed has co-authored four previous books, including *When Everyone Leads* and *For the Common Good.*

Amanda Cebula is an Adjunct Instructor at Kansas State University. She served as the director of project development and business development at the Kansas Leadership Center from 2012-2017.

About the Illustrator

Pat Byrnes is best know for his cartoons in *The New Yorker.* He is a winner of the National Cartoonists Society "Silver Reuben" Award. His illustrations appear in *Your Leadership Edge* and *When Everyone Leads.* He lives with his family on the banks of the Chicago River.

Notes

KLC Press

Visit our website at kansasleadershipcenter.org

Printed in the United States of America

Design by Stauber Brand Studio
Copy editing by Shannon Littlejohn

Kansas Leadership Center
325 E. Douglas Avenue
Wichita, Kansas 67202 USA
316.712.4950

www.ingramcontent.com/pod-product-compliance
Lightning Source LLC
LaVergne TN
LVHW070913210926
848482LV00017B/1065
9781959472049